THE FASHIONABLE FIRE PLACE
1660 · 1840

CHRISTOPHER GILBERT
ANTHONY WELLS-COLE

CONTENTS

'OF CHIMNEY-PIECES'   5

CHIMNEYPIECES
AT TEMPLE NEWSAM   13

FIRE FURNITURE   21

    Fire grates   22

    Fenders and guards   29

    Fire irons   31

    Hearth brushes and brooms   37

    Bellows   37

    Coal boxes and coal scuttles   41

    Cats   42

    Trivets   43

    Chair back screens   44

    Chimney boards   46

PRINTED AND
MANUSCRIPT DESIGNS   51

    Designs by smiths and ironmongers   51

    Designs by furniture makers   59

    Designs by architects   59

STOVE GRATE MAKERS   61

ABRAHAM BUZAGLO   63

THE CARRON IRON COMPANY
AND THE
COALBROOKDALE COMPANY   66

JUTSHAM'S CARLTON HOUSE
DAYBOOK 1806–29   70

'SUITES OF
CHIMNEY ORNAMENTS'   72

FACING PAGE

Frontispiece to John Crunden's
The Chimneypiece Maker's Daily Assistant, 1766,
engraved by R. Pranker after Isaac Taylor

FOREWORD

During the 1970s a notable series of exhibitions was staged at Temple Newsam House which explored, for the first time, regional styles in 17th-century oak furniture and focused on sub-groups within the Georgian and Victorian vernacular tradition. Attention has now shifted to aspects of country house interiors — another neglected field of research which it is hoped to illuminate in a programme of studies. Last year's project devoted to historic paper hangings attracted widespread interest and this exhibition concentrates on the place of the chimneypiece and fire furniture in fashionable room schemes. Further booklets on floor treatments, window draperies, lighting and, possibly, picture hangs are planned.

It would obviously be impossible to assemble such an impressive array of material without the co-operation of colleagues in the museum profession, private collectors, fellow scholars and various well-wishers. Our best thanks are due to everyone who has lent items for the present display; they are named in the catalogue entries, but others deserve a special mention for their encouragement, support and information supplied. They include Robert Aagaard, Ros Allwood, Michael Archer, Geoffrey de Bellaigue, Claude Blair, Timothy Clifford, John Cornforth, T. Crowther & Son Ltd, R. N. Dean, Martin Drury, Oliver Fairclough, Anton Gabszewicz, J. D. Galbraith, Ian Gow, John Hardy, Graham Hood, A. Hunter, John Jacob, V. J. Kite, James Lomax, John Lord, Sally MacDonald, John Mallet, Peter Marlow, John Powell, Miss P. Rogers, J. M. Sanderson, Jacob Simon, Mark Suggit, Eric Till, Maurice Tomlin, Richard Wakeford, Rory Wardroper, Michael Wilson, Lucy Wood.

We are also grateful to the following for allowing us to illustrate items from their collections: Bath Public Libraries, Boston Public Library (the Wiggin Collection), the Trustees of the British Museum, the Trustees of the National Gallery and of the Victoria & Albert Museum, the Colonial Williamsburg Foundation, the National Trust and Edinburgh Record Office. We also acknowledge the kindness of Lady Monson in allowing us to quote from the Monson papers deposited with the Lincolnshire Archives Office, and of Messrs. Christie for permission to quote from the 1781 Christie & Ansell catalogue of Wedgwood and Bentley's stock.

Finally we wish to thank the Paul Mellon Centre for Studies in British Art (London) Ltd, for making a generous grant towards the cost of photography for this handbook.

COUNCILLOR ELIZABETH NASH
Chairman, Leisure Services Committee

CHRISTOPHER GILBERT
Director of Art Galleries

LITERATURE AND FURTHER READING

A. CONTEMPORARY VIEWS OF INTERIORS, ETC.

P. Agius
Ackermann's Regency Furniture and Interiors, 1984

J. Cornforth
English Interiors 1790–1848. The Quest for Comfort, 1978

R. Edwards
Early Conversation Pictures, 1954

J. Fowler and J. Cornforth
English Decoration in the 18th Century, 1974

M. Girouard
Life in the English Country House, 1978

John Morley
The Making of the Royal Pavilion, Brighton, 1984

M. Praz
Conversation Pieces, 1971

S. Sitwell
Conversation Pieces, 1936

P. K. Thornton
Seventeenth Century Interior Decoration in England, France & Holland, 1981

P. K. Thornton
Authentic Decor: The Domestic Interior 1620–1920, 1984

P. K. Thornton and M. F. Tomlin
The Furnishing and Decoration of Ham House, 1980

B. FIRE FURNITURE AND CHIMNEY ORNAMENTS

M. Archer
'Delft at Dyrham', *National Trust Yearbook 1975–76*

R. H. Campbell
Carron Company, 1961

Connoisseur Period Guide
Regency, 1810–30

D. J. Eveleigh
Firegrates and Ranges, 1983

R. Gentle
English Domestic Brass, 1975

N. Goodison
Ormolu: The work of Matthew Boulton, 1974

W. D. John and K. Coombes
Paktong, 1970

A. Kelly
Decorative Wedgwood, 1965

A. Kelly
The Book of English Fireplaces, 1968

A. Laing
Lighting, 1982

J. Seymour Lindsay
Iron & Brass Implements & the English House, 1925

R. Lister
Decorative Cast Ironwork in Great Britain, 1960

N. Fletcher Little
'Pictures on the Hearth', *Country Life*, 4 January 1973

B. Reade
Regency Antiques, 1953

H. P. and N. Schiffer
Antique Iron, 1979

D. Stillman
The Decorative Works of Robert Adam, 1966

'As the Egyptians, the Greeks, and the Romans, to whom architecture is so much indebted in other respects, lived in warm climates, where fires in the apartments were seldom or never necessary, they have thrown but few lights on this branch of architecture.'

So William Chambers begins his account of chimneypieces in his *Treatise on Civil Architecture* first published in 1759, and his comments show the preoccupations of one of the leading 18th-century British architects. His first concern, as a neoclassical architect, is to establish a classical authority for the chimneypiece and he quotes two Italians, Scamozzi and Palladio. The origins of the classical chimneypiece in England, however, are to be found in the books of architecture of Sebastiano Serlio (1475–1554); Book IV was published first in Venice in 1537, was quickly translated from Italian into many languages and used as a source of designs. The chimneypieces in the hall at Wollaton in Nottinghamshire (from Book IV) and at Burghley House near Stamford, Hardwick Hall and Bolsover Castle, Derbyshire (from Book VII), are well known but several other instances could be cited. The standard Elizabethan and Jacobean kind of chimneypiece that Chambers describes as 'composed of a projecting entablature, supported by consoles, termini [terms], or caryatides' was also derived from designs by Jacques Androuet Du Cerceau (1515–c.1584; his *Second Livre d'Architecture* 1561 provided numerous designs), Jan Vredeman de Vries (1526–1604) and Wendel Dietterlin (1551–99) whose *Architectura* published from 1593 was known to English architect-masons including the Smythsons.

'Neither the Italians nor the French, nor indeed any of the continental nations have ever excelled in compositions of chimney-pieces. I believe we may justly consider Inigo Jones as the first who arrived at any great degree of perfection in this material branch of the art.' Here Chambers is less than fair or indeed accurate. Not only does he ignore chimneypieces at Fontainebleau or Ecouen, Chenonceaux or Blois, but he passes over the fact that, as Palladio published no designs for chimneypieces in *I Quattri Libri dell'Architettura* of 1570, Jones was obliged to adapt the printed designs of his somewhat younger French contemporaries, Jean Barbet (1591–before 1654) and Jean Cotelle (1607–76). Some of the rooms of the Queens House at Greenwich must have had quite an up-to-date French look.

As a serious-minded classicist Chambers was apparently not interested (at least in this brief account) in the work of, for instance, Sir Roger Pratt, who apparently used Vignola's *Regola delli cinque ordini* 1620 for chimneypieces at Coleshill in Berkshire (1650–1662), nor indeed of Sir John Vanburgh and Nicholas Hawksmoor, although Sir John merits a back-hander later on. His 1836 editor, J. B. Papworth, clearly admired late Stuart interiors, for in a footnote he writes, 'In England, Gibbs, and the architects of his time, increased [the chimneypiece's] magnitude, and multiplied its embellishments, calling in the aid of sculpture, painting, and carving, to the last of which, the celebrated Grinlin Gibbon added very curious efforts of the gouge and chisel'. While he telescoped time somewhat misleadingly — Grinling Gibbons, of course, was contemporary with Wren, and collaborated with him in major projects (adding ornament to Wren's architecture, for instance, in a number of drawings in the Soane Museum) — Papworth is right in that James Gibbs (1682–1754) and other architects of his time gave the chimneypiece particular importance. Gibbs's *Book of Architecture* (1728, second edition 1739), William Kent's *Designs of Inigo Jones, with some Additional Designs* [by Lord Burlington] 1727, and John Vardy's *Some Designs of Mr Inigo Jones and Mr William Kent* 1744, were very influential publications. Their stylistic differences, which seem important in an age of classification such as ours, went unremarked and were avidly plundered by Edward Hoppus (*The Gentleman's and Builder's Repository* 1737) or Batty Langley (*Treasury of Designs* 1750), designs by Kent and Gibbs often appearing side by side, usually unattributed. Chambers was aware of their importance for he writes: 'Others of our English architects have, since [Jones's] time, wrought upon his ideas, or furnished good inventions of their own; and England being at present possessed of many ingenious and able sculptors, of whom one chief employment is to execute magnificent chimney-pieces, now happily much in vogue, it may be said, that in this particular we surpass all other nations, not only in point of expense, but likewise in taste of design, and excellence of workmanship'. Sculptors of the generation of Kent included Rysbrack, whose chimneypieces at Houghton Hall, Norfolk, Clandon Park, Surrey, and elsewhere are well-known, and Sir Henry Cheere, twenty-eight of whose chimneypiece designs are in the Victoria & Albert Museum. Space and, no doubt, inclination precluded him from mentioning those who, like Cheere, worked in the rococo manner for stylistically they must have been an anathema to him. These included architects (among them Peter Glazier, William and John Halfpenny, Robert Morris, Timothy Lightoler and Sir Robert Taylor — those of Abraham Swan in his *Chimneypieces* 1748 and even more *The British Architect* 1738 are particularly fine), cabinetmakers or general upholders (Thomas Chippendale, Matthias Lock, and the Linnells) and a host of house-carvers, known by name like Richard Fisher of York or Luke Lightfoot, or else completely anonymous.

On the whole-page spread illustrating chimneypiece design Chambers selects two by Palladio and supplies the rest himself. There is no mention of Robert Adam, for Chambers despised his taste and ensured his exclusion from the Royal Academy, but J. B. Papworth mentions a man who inspired both the rivals: 'The published works of Piranese [Giovanni Battista Piranesi, 1720–78] also exhibit the interest taken in his day in behalf of this department of art, by some of our nobility, for under their patronage he was induced to make the sumptuous designs for chimney-pieces which embellish one of his volumes'. This was his *Diverse Maniere d'Adornare i Cammini* 1769 and amongst his patrons were Lord Exeter at Burghley House, and John Hope, father of Thomas Hope, who himself became a patron, collector and designer. His *Household Furniture and Interior Decoration* 1807 illustrated the objects and interiors he had created in his house in Duchess Street, amongst them some chimneypieces which are both individual and exciting.

'The size of the chimney must depend on the dimensions of the room wherein it is placed' and Chambers specifies the sizes: 'In the smallest apartments, the width of the aperture is never made less than from three feet to three feet six inches' and so on. His criteria become clear when he says '. . . should the room be extremely large (as is frequently the case of halls, galleries, and saloons), and one chimney of these last dimensions neither afford sufficient heat to warm the room, nor sufficient space round it for the company, it will be much more convenient, and far handsomer, to have two chimney-pieces of a moderate size, than a single one exceedingly large, all the parts of which would appear clumsy and disproportioned to the other decorations of the room'. He opens on a point of what we would call etiquette: 'The chimney should always be situated so as to be immediately seen by those who enter, that they may not have the persons already in the room, who are generally seated about the fire, to search for'. He could hardly have expressed better the difference between what Mark Girouard has called the Formal house and the Social house, the increasing informality of life towards the end of the century.

'The middle of the side partition wall is the properest place in halls, saloons, and other rooms of passage, to which the principal entrances are commonly in the middle of the front, or of the back wall; but in drawing-rooms, dressing-rooms, and the like, the middle of the back wall is the best situation, the chimney being then furthest removed from the doors of communication. The case is the same with respect to galleries and libraries, whose doors are generally at one or both ends. In bed-chambers, the chimney is always placed in the middle of one of the side partition walls; and in closets, or other very small places, it is, to save room, sometimes placed in one corner.'

Chambers also warns against the Italian (and French) practice of putting the chimneypiece between windows on an outside wall, not only because that position concentrates most of the interest of the room on that wall but also because the chimneys have to be carried up that much further unsupported, which makes them 'very liable to be blown down'. He also recommends that, if possible, the flues should be taken up in the thickness of the wall to obviate the chimney breast and the consequent break in the entablature of the room.

Just as the position of chimneypieces was governed by the function of their room, so was their appearance: 'Their ornaments consists of architraves, friezes, cornices, columns, pilasters, termini, caryatides, consoles, and all kind of ornaments of sculpture, representing animal or vegetable productions of nature; likewise vases, paterae, trophies of various kinds, and instruments or symbols of religion, arts, arms, letters, and commerce. In designing them, regard must be had to the nature of the place where they are to be employed. Such as are intended for halls, guard-rooms, saloons, galleries and other considerable places, must be composed of large parts, few in number, of distinct and simple forms, and having a a bold relief; but chimney-pieces for drawing rooms, dressing-rooms, bed-chambers, and such like, may be of a more delicate and complicated composition. The workmanship of all chimney-pieces must be perfectly well finished, like all other objects liable to close inspection; and the ornaments, figures, and profiles, both in form, proportions and quantity, must be suited to the other parts of the room, and be allusive to the uses for which it is intended'. That Chambers practised what he preached is evidence in his decoration of the eating room at Osterley Park, Middlesex; and when Robert Adam replaced him as architect there he continued to make decoration symbolic of the function of rooms.

Earlier generations were clearly thicker-skinned than the sophisticated generation of Chambers and Wedgwood. Chambers continues, 'All nudities and indecent representations must be avoided, both in chimney-pieces and in every other ornament of apartments to which children, ladies, and other modest, grave persons, have constant recourse, [what would Bess of Hardwick, whose bedchamber had a pair of grotesquely nude caryatid figures on the chimneypiece, have made of this?] together with all representations capable of exciting horror, grief, disgust, or any gloomy, unpleasing situations'. Chambers here reiterates objections made by Isaac Ware some years before and Wedgwood expressed much the same misgivings when he wrote to Flaxman: 'There is one objection which I am afraid is insurmountable, and that is the nakedness of the figures. To clothe them would not only be a great increase of labour, but would require the hand of an experienced master in the art, and, besides, the pieces would not then be a copy of the antique. I know the nudities might be covered with leaves but that is not enough. The same objection applies to the *Judgment of Paris* and the other pieces; and indeed the mode is so general in the work of the ancients that it will be very difficult to avoid the introduction of naked figures. On the other hand it is absolutely necessary to do so, or to keep the pieces for our own use, for none, either male or female will take or apply them as furniture, if the figures are naked'. As Alison Kelly remarks, Wedgwood seems to have forgotten all about it, for the designs went into production, and were used in chimneypieces without any difficulty.

Chambers next turns briefly to materials: 'Chimney-pieces are made either of stone, of marble, or of a mixture of these, with wood, scagliola, or-moulu or some other unfragile substances'. He alludes, in passing, to costs which he may have felt to be irrelevant to his readers (although we know the wealthiest patrons could be the most tight-fisted): 'Those of marble are most costly, but they are also most elegant, and the only ones used in highly finished apartments, where they are seen either of white or variegated marbles, sometimes inlaid and decorated with the materials just mentioned. All their ornaments, figures, or profiles, are to be made of the pure white sort, but their friezes, tablets, panels, shafts of columns, and other plain parts, may be of particoloured marbles, such as the yellow of Siena, the brocatello of Spain, the jaspers of Sicily, and many other modern as well as antique marbles, frequently to be had in England. Festoons of flowers, trophies, and foliages, frets and other such decorations, cut in white statuary marble, and fixed on grounds of these, have a very good effect. But there should never be above two, or, at the utmost, three different sorts of colours in the same chimney-piece, all brilliant, and harmonising with each other'.

Though Chambers writes in the late 1760s, marble had from the beginning of our period always been the most expensive material. At Kiveton Park near Sheffield, a house built between 1697 and 1705, the purple marble chimneypieces of the Great Dining Room and the Hall, at £23 and £27 respectively, were valued at more than twice the price of the 'Light Culler deavonshire marble' of the bed chamber and the 'Sad Cullerd Devonshire marble' of the Drawing Room (both were described as 'Plimouth' in the 1727 inventory). In several rooms at Kiveton table tops were made *en suite* as they were in the Marble Dining Room at Ham House where the material was grey and white marble. In 1743 Horace Walpole described the 'Salon' at Houghton Hall in Norfolk as having 'Chimney and tables of Black and Gold marble'. *The Builders Dictionary* published in 1734 reported that Egyptian (black-streaked) or Rome (liver-coloured) marble chimneypieces cost between £12 and £14, stone ones could be had for between 10 and 40 s according to the amount of ornament, while wooden ones were priced between 10 and 20 s and could be painted for 2 s extra. The marble and stone ones must have been comparatively simple because Henry Cheere charged 100 gns for the drawing room chimneypiece at Ditchley House, Oxfordshire, in 1739, £100 for those in the 'little room within the Great Room' and in the Velvet Room, and £84 for the Tapestry Room. Rysbrack's India Office relief, in the overmantel, cost £100 in 1730, and he charged £266 15s for a chimney piece at Longford Castle in 1744, though two others six years earlier totalled £57 14s. Prices remained

Fig. 1a Delftware pyramid flower pot at Dyrham Park.

The National Trust

much the same throughout the century: in 1769 Lord Monson bought, apparently for Burton Hall near Lincoln [Monson papers, 11/9],

a Veined and Statuary Marble Chimney piece set up in Breakfast room	£77
Do intire Staty. in the Drawing room	£109 10s
Do in the Dining room	£126
Do. Veined in the Hall	£29

Ten years later he paid James Paine the younger £100 13s 9d for a drawing room chimneypiece, while in 1789 John Bacon senior charged £266 13s for the white marble chimneypiece in the Music Room at Heaton (its grate, by Brodie and Young of Blackfriars, cost £41 4s). Hearths were generally made of the same marble or stone as the chimneypiece and were usually the same width. Any difference in dimensions may indicate some alteration. Only in exceptional circumstances were they decorated. A mid 16th-century one at Lacock Abbey in Wiltshire is inlaid with metal, some post-Restoration ones at Burghley House have geometric patterns in black and white marble, the scagliola chimneypiece in the Queens Closet at Ham House has a scagliola hearth to match. Stephen Wright's drawing (in the Victoria & Albert Museum) for a chimneypiece at Clumber has a hearth inlaid with a Greek key pattern in a contrasting colour, but it was apparently not executed. Raised marble curbs around the edge of the hearth stone are mostly modern but at least one old one survives made for Hampton Court, Herefordshire, but never used there; are they curbs that are described in William Moreton's invoice to Lady Saunderson in 1730 for 'Macking two marble Fenders'? [Monson 12].

In other materials chimneypieces came much cheaper. John West 'at the Cabinet in King's Street Covent Garden' charged a Mrs Morse £11 25s for 'A Neat carv'd Chimney in the Chinese Taste' on Christmas Eve 1752 and supplied a white-painted and gilt pier glass frame to match. Thomas Chippendale himself occasionally supplied chimneypieces, in 1760 invoicing Sir William Robinson for 'a very large Glass-border'd Chimney-piece richly carv'd & gilt in burnish'd-gold wt a Pediment top & a large oval glass in the middle £48'.

Stylistic change must have made all but the wealthiest owners shudder with alarm. If they were determined to move with the times there were several possible alternatives to buying expensive new marble chimneypieces. In 1781 Chippendale, Haig & Co charged Sir Gilbert Heathcote 5s 6d for 'Men's time taking off the large gilt ornaments of the 2 Chymney Pieces, and £10 18s for Finish the pilasters — and moldings with additional new ornaments — and making very neat carvd antique ornaments to the frizes of the 2 chymney pieces — and fixing them compt'. Or a simple pine chimneypiece in the neoclassical manner could be very inexpensive. The same firm supplied in 1778 'A neat deal mantlepiece with Tablet and neat carved Ornaments on

do painted white, for Blue paper Bedchamber at North End and a Man there fixing do', charging £1 19s.

Otherwise the small scale and low relief ornament of the neoclassical style lent itself ideally to replication by inexpensive methods. Plaster or composition ornament was produced from boxwood or metal moulds in places as widely spread as Birmingham, Bristol, London, even Grantham in Lincolnshire, making the cost of a complete chimneypiece in 1796 between £1 and £6 according to size; loose ornaments cost between 5s and 30s the set. Birmingham manufacturers sold die-stamped white alloy ornaments, described in the catalogue of one company, Jee, Eginton & Co:

No 303 | Chimney-piece complete | The numbers on the Chimney-piece refer to the single Ornaments, engraved full size: & are sold separate or compleat. | Their Elegance, Duration, & Cheapness, are best recommended by a comparison with other Carvings.

Matthew Boulton made some chimneypiece ornaments in pewter, and occasionally in ormolu, charging Sir Robert Cunliffe £19 1s for a pair of gilt figures for a chimneypiece in 1774. But one of the most successful manufacturers was Wedgwood. The sale of his stock in 1781 included

BAS RELIEFS, in Jasper, for CHIMNEY-PIECES, &c . . . [lot] 38 A suite for a Chimney-piece, in *fine white Porcelain bisque*: Tablet, *Triumph of Bacchus*; Frieze, *Hope, Pythagoras reading, a Sacrifice to Peace, and a Muse recording a Victory*; Blocks, *Spring and Autumn*

It realised £3. Wedgwood also made a number of complete chimneypieces and so did the Coade factory, which had a range of thirty designs costing between 25 s and 14 gns.

Sir William Chambers is, surprisingly, silent on a matter which remained a preoccupation throughout the period — smoky chimneys. The French architect Philibert de l'Orme (c. 1505–70) had invented ingenious gadgets to hang within the flue to prevent downdraughts, the *Builders Dictionary* published in 1734 devotes several paragraphs to it and Ackermann's *Repository* nearly a hundred years later reported on new devices to obviate 'this evil [which] has engaged the thoughts of Dr Franklin and some of the most eminent philosophers'.

Chambers liked to supervise every aspect of his interiors so we might expect him to recommend what kind of paintings to hang over the chimney piece. Instead we have to go to inventories and other sources of information. William Winde, who was remodelling Castle Bromwich Hall in 1688 wrote: 'As to ye pictures for ye chymeny peece in ye Dining roome yr Ladp is left at liberty. Either to have figures or Landschipe, but according to ye Strickte rule of adorning of Roomes it ought to [be] pleasant and of a bright coloring as ye painting . . .'. The 1727 inventory of Kiveton Park also provides valuable information: 'I Picture of King Charles ye 2*d*. on Horsback, in Carved Frame fix'd over ye Chimney, a Carved ffreez pannel underneath . . .' in The Great Dining Room; 'I Chimney Glass fix'd in Red & Gold Japan fra. [me] I Whole Length of a Nun fix'd over Chimney', in the Best Dressing Room. Indeed of the overmantel paintings mentioned, eight were portraits and two were landscapes. Three were mentioned in the Marquis of Carmarthen's house at Thorp Salvin that year, two being landscapes, the other in the Drawing Room a 'piece of Ruins'. Antonio Ioli painted such a piece for one of the overmantels in the Saloon at Temple Newsam and provided a cityscape, Rome, for the other. The *Builder's Dictionary*, under Disposition of Pictures, advised hanging '. . . upon Chimney-Pieces, only Land-skips; for they chiefly adorn'. And Sir Gilbert Heathcote of Normanton, Rutland, was invoiced for £25 by Isaac Gosset in August 1770 'for a Landskip Chemony Picture' and 'for a frame for it £9 16*s*'. Mr and Mrs Richard Bull had a landscape over their chimneypiece in Essex (if we can believe Arthur Devis) but a census of contemporary views would probably reveal that classical scenes were more commonly hung there. While architects from the time of Colen Campbell in the early 18th century had illustrated rooms in 'exploded' views with their walls laid flat, and had taken pains to integrate picture frames into their overall scheme there are not always signs that owners took their recommendations to heart: pictures might be hung high or low, in arrangements which were not always symmetrical, sometimes they are not hung at all (Cat. 69); looking-glasses were the most usual substitute but sometimes their place was taken by arms and armour (Fig. 1b).

Chambers did not need to tell his contemporaries what kinds of ornaments were suitable for use on chim-neypieces although he had designed some himself for Matthew Boulton and Josiah Wedgwood; so some of the possibilities are described in a separate section. His only comments about how people felt about the chimneypiece are oblique (' . . . persons already in the room, who are generally seated about the fire . . .' and 'sufficient space round it for the company . . .') but make it clear that in

Fig. 1b J. G. Haid after John Zoffany, 'Mr Foote as Major Sturgeon'.
The Trustees of the British Museum

England the fireplace was the natural focus of life, in a way which it was not always in other countries. Talking of a piece of furniture for the centre of a room called the *faineante* or idler — a kind of *chaise-longue* — Ackermann's *Repository* said in May 1823: 'This piece of furniture is suited to the manners of the French; it is a substitute for the fire-place with us, as it becomes the rallying point or conversational centre: here the lady of the mansion seats herself, and here receives her friends; they assemble round her, and thus the party is collected into a group, occupying the middle of the apartment'.

Contemporary views throughout the period show people drawn up to the fire for light as well as warmth. Brilliant reflective materials were used to reflect the firelight as in the Duke of Chandos's house at Cannons, in Middlesex, where John Loveday noted in June 1733 'Silver bottoms and cheeks to the Chiminies', and at Sir Gregory Page's house in Blackheath in 1739 'the Chimney-pieces . . . so elegant; and the bottoms and cheeks of two Chimnies are entirely of Brass; there are such of silver at Cannons'. Some form of lighting was almost always associated with the chimney-breast. In the late 17th century sconces of various materials were used. At Dyrham in 1702 and again in 1710 there were recorded '*Gilt Leather Parlor* A looking Glass & 2 Glass Sconces ov^r ye Chimney' and the Terras Bed Chamber and Mrs Anne Blathwayte's Bed Chamber both had 'a pr. of Japan Sconces'. At Kiveton in 1727 the North East Bedchamber had '2 Chimney Sconces Carved & Gilded' while the South East Drawing Room had '6 Glass Sconces wth Brass Nossles, Silver'd. 2 ffor ye Chimney Do'. Amongst several others those of the North East Drawing Room were the most elaborate: '3 Large Glass Sconces wth. purple & Gold Glass frames & double brass Sockets Silver'd. 2 Chimney Sconces Do'.

During the Palladian phase of the early 18th century, lighting continued in England to be separate from the chimneypiece and overmantel, though no doubt candlesticks were placed over the chimney. Elaborate carved and gilt wall sconces were made, like the two at Temple Newsam from a set attributed to Benjamin Goodison, or the pair made for the saloon by James Pascall in 1745. Such lively rococo compositions are parodied in Hogarth's *Marriage à la Mode* (see front cover), where the two-branch candle sconce consists of naturalistically treated foliage in which nest a clock, a cat, two fish and a Buddha. Increasingly, however, England followed a lead from France and incorporated lighting into the design of the overmantel mirror and this became very common around the middle of the century.

The classical-style garniture which became *de rigueur* from the late 1760s often incorporated vases adaptable as candelabra or objects designed primarily for lighting purposes: Wedgwood made both producing basalt or jasperware bases to be made up, with ormolu fittings and glass lustres, as candelabra (Cat. 70). Needless to say Mrs Coade made them as well (Cat. 73). In 1795 Harewood House had, for instance:

White Drawing Room . . . Two Glass Jerandoles upon the Chimney Piece
Saloon . . . 4 Jerandoles with 3 Branches each upon the [two] chimneypieces

and so on. Meanwhile at Audley House two years later the library is specified as having '2 Argands Lamps' on the chimneypiece and these quickly proved themselves a more efficient means of lighting than candles. Nonetheless oil-burning lamps like those made for the Duke of Newcastle at Clumber Park (Cat. 76) never entirely replaced candelabra which remained indispensible components of the adornment of the chimney piece during the Regency period.

The formal manner in which furniture was disposed around the walls for most of the 18th century in England, familiar from plates in *Vitruvius Britannicus* from 1715 onwards, contrasts dramatically with contemporary views showing rooms in use. Hogarth's painting of the Assembly at Wanstead shows the company divided into several groups seated around the fireplace drinking tea or playing cards. The recently-married couple in his *Marriage à la Mode* (see front cover) slouch at the breakfast table which is drawn up close to the lighted fire, but it was probably more usual to have it placed slightly to one side. Fire-screens protected people, and other furniture, from being scorched. Sometime around 1800, the date of a proposal for a drawing room in England (Thornton 1984, pl. 186), furniture was deliberately placed out in the room instead of ranged around the walls, resulting in the arrangement of chairs or sofas facing each other in front of the fireplace that is so familiar in country houses today. The family were certainly prepared, in the 1780s, to pull furniture around to get people into groups, but privacy was increasingly sought after and the servants, who must previously have done most of the rearranging, were more and more banished to their own quarters. So a French visitor to Osterley Park in 1810–11 noted that 'Tables, sofas, and chairs were studiously derangès about the fireplaces, and in the middle of the rooms, as if the family had just left them'.

The change was decisive. Once the owner broke the stranglehold of the architect in the disposition of furniture, rooms, and in particular fireplaces, became increasingly cluttered. The Saloon at Harewood in 1795 had three different types of fire-screen: '– Fire Screens with Blue & Gold Stands, 2 Folding Fire Screens, and one Face Do', the latter possibly one of the hand-held variety. The chimney breast significantly became the normal position for bell pulls: at Temple Newsam they were all listed in the 1808 inventory.

During the summer months, with no need for a fire, the fireplace was often completely ignored, chairs being drawn up to it as if it wasn't there. The opening was often blocked off with a chimney board (and these are discussed separately), sometimes painted with a vase of flowers: several are known and more probably survive

Fig. 1c James Gillray 'TEMPERANCE enjoying a Frugal Meal' 1792

The Trustees of the British Museum

masquerading, as perhaps at Burghley, as decorative flower paintings. These reflect the practice, common from the 17th century onwards of removing the grate during the summer and substituting a vase, preferably of oriental blue and white porcelain or European delftware. Three jars are shown on the hearth in Daniel Marot's design for a porcelain room for Queen Mary at Hampton Court; his design for a state bedchamber in Holland of *c.* 1703 has two jars and a tub on a stand, with an orange or myrtle bush growing in it; in another design for a porcelain room he had no fewer than eight objects in the fire place.

This was not just a designer's whim. William Blathwayt's Dyrham Park, near Bath, had no fewer than nine rooms with a 'delf flower pott in ye Chimney'. First listed in 1703, they were still there in 1742 and many still survive. They were intended to have plants growing in them, myrtle, orange and bay trees cultivated in the Orangery attached to the house. Two rooms in 1710 had 'A large Pyramid Delft Flower pot in ye Chimney' and these are still in the house (Fig. 1a).

Despite the fact that most of the 18th century inventories of Temple Newsam were taken during the summer months there is evidence neither of vases of flowers nor of chimney boards but there is plenty of evidence that the placing of vases (with or without flowers or shrubs) was common, in paintings by William Hogarth, Arthur Devis, Gawen Hamilton, Edward Haytley, Francis Hayman and John Zoffany (Fig. 1b). That the practice was not merely an owner's fancy but had the sanction even of a strict Palladian architect is proved by William Kent's illustration of one of John Gay's *Fables*, (number 18) 'The Painter who pleased nobody and everybody' published in 1727.

Flowers or plants continued to be put in the fireplace during the second half of the 18th century, Wedgwood describing to Bentley in 1772 'Bough-pots for a hearth'. But the introduction of fixed grates made it more difficult: in the 1780s Mary Turner Hog had to stick tongs through the bars of the grate itself (in a painting by David Allan) and in 1792 Gillray showed a vase of flowers actually in the grate (Fig. 1c). This was hardly satisfactory and instead a 'fire-paper' folded into a fan shape might be placed there: one is visible in a mid 19th-century photograph of a country house in Ireland (Thornton 1984, pl. 416).

Very occasionally other objects occupied the fireplace when the fire was not lit: a wine cooler for a feast in Bologna in 1693, or a library globe. Certainly the most eccentric of all was in that extraordinary house, A la Ronde, near Exmouth, built in the 1790s for the Miss Parminsters, who had been inspired by S. Vitale in Ravenna. In the fireplace of the dining room is a shell-work grotto, made by the ladies themselves, which in winter was lifted out complete so that the fireplace could be used.

CHIMNEYPIECES AT TEMPLE NEWSAM

Temple Newsam has been both fortunate and unfortunate with its chimneypieces: amongst those that survive are some of the most magnificent mid 18th-century examples in England, but many others have been superseded by ones more in the current style, themselves replaced or removed in later years. From this point of view the lowest ebb was reached during the 1930s and '40s: faced with the threat of war and the need to provide as much wall space at Temple Newsam for paintings evacuated there from the City Art Gallery, the Director, Philip Hendy, took several chimneypieces out, boarded and papered over where they had been. The chimneypieces were either sold, or dismantled and kept in the cellars where they deteriorated through damp. Measures are now under way to reinstate them where possible or to provide appropriate ones from other sources, but these have been delayed through lack of funds.

From the early Tudor house of Thomas Lord Darcy several fireplaces with the typical four-centred arch survive, only one now visible in a part of the house open to the public. This heated the principal apartment of the early 16th-century palace, on the second floor of the West Wing (now called the Tudor or Bretton room) but the panelling and overmantel now associated with it do not belong, being brought in from Bretton Hall near Wakefield and St Ives, Bingley, since the Second World War. Nothing remains of what must have been one of the principal chimneypieces, in the Great Hall, for this was on the south wall and was removed in alterations in 1796 if not before. It may anyway have been replaced in the time of Sir Arthur Ingram who bought Temple Newsam in 1622, for he found the north and south wings in a state of decay and had to rebuild them. From the accounts (belonging to West Yorkshire Archives Service at Sheepscar, Leeds) chimneypieces were supplied over an eight-year period from 1629 when four wooden ones were sent, probably from York, where Sir Arthur and several of his masons and plasterers lived. His 150-ft Long Gallery was being provided with chimneypieces in 1634–35 and traces of plasterwork painted with strapwork (revealed when the present Gallery was being rehung in 1940) may have had something to do with them. The house had at least 38 chimneys (and probably more than that number of flues) as three workmen were paid for finishing them in 1636. On 24 February that year there was a catastrophic fire which seems to have destroyed much of the south and perhaps east wing: Sir Arthur and his steward rode over from York in two hours to survey the damage, and the family's sensitivity to the problem is shown by the payment that November 'For an iron range for Sir Thomas Ingram's chamber [probably in the south-east corner] at Temple Newsam being fearful of the fire, weight 97 lbs @ 3d lb = 12/-'.

Most of the payments in 1636 and 1637 were to Thomas Ventris, father and son: the father was paid £3 for two chimneypieces in the 'Drawing Chamber next best chamber in the Gallery' and 11s 8d for 'timber and making a chimney piece in Sir Thomas Ingram's chamber'; there was a payment of 12s for 'Timber Thos Ventris, Junr, had for the 1st chimney piece' while the decorative painter John Carleton invoiced 'for 3 yds of cloth he bought for pictures for Ventris first chimneypiece = 3/9'. Finally, the son was paid 'to clear for making for the 3 chimney pieces at Temple Newsam = £4–16–8, making £13–6–8'.

In view of this documentary evidence it is all the more disappointing that none of these chimneypieces survive, although early 17th-century examples at Sherriff Hutton, another of Sir Arthur's houses, and in Coney Street, York, where the Ventris family had their workshop, may be similar. Nonetheless, lengths of moulded floral plasterwork with gilding, forming two friezes totalling nearly seven feet in depth, survive on the fireplace wall in what is now known as the Darnley Room, above areas of plasterwork on the chimney breast marbled in pink and blue.

Sir Arthur died in 1642 and little was done to the house before the inventory taken at the death of his grandson Henry, 1st Viscount Irwin, in 1666. This records twelve rooms as having either 'chimney pictures' or a picture 'for' or 'over' the chimney. Most if not all these were presumably built in to panelling. There is also the implication that the chimney picture was the only one in the majority of rooms. In 'my Lords Dressinge Rooms' there was 'a blew curtaine over the Chimney' and 'an old Mapp'. Hearth tax returns for the 1670s show that there were forty-five hearths in the house.

The next indication of work in progress comes with the bill from Henry Long in 1684 for painting amongst other things 'the Stone Chymney peece in ye Hall'; the one in the dining room was also painted at a cost of £1 9s 4d. An inventory taken the next year records in the 'Best Lodging Roome[s] . . . Three marble Chymney pieces'. None of these apparently survives.

In the 1680s Queen Mary and her architect Daniel Marot initiated a taste in England for the massing of Chinese porcelain in specially created rooms, concentrating it particularly over the chimneypiece on specially constructed stands. It was a fashion which even the relatively unartistic 3rd Viscount Irwin, or his wife, quickly followed. The inventory taken on his death in 1702 records 'In the Damask Chamber . . . 2 corner shelfs of cheyna ware & over ye chimney. In the Clossett . . . I Iron stove Grate . . . 2 sconces [for candles] china ware over the chimney'. His successor, the 4th Viscount, by the time of his death in 1714 had added 'In ye

Fig. 2 One of the two chimneypieces made for the Saloon by Robert Doe

Fig. 3 William Kent's design, published by John Vardy

withdrawing room . . . [one cabinett with Chinea upon itt] . . . some chinea over ye chimney piece'. Whoever it was that inventoried his brother's goods in 1721 listed picturesquely 'Mohaire roome . . . 2 Candle Stickes and Chinay over Chimley . . .' in the Dressing roome . . . Chiney upon the Chimney and under the Cabinett', besides that in three other rooms. We are given some idea of the quantities involved in the inventory of 1734:

> The Drawing Room . . . 80 pieces of China upon Chimney
>
> The Mohair . . . Some China Over Chimney (to wit) 18 pieces of different Sorts, some broke
>
> The Dressing Room next Adjoining . . . 17 China pieces of divers Sorts 5 Charr potts
>
> The Damask Room . . . 70 Pieces of China upon the Chimney-piece & in the 2 Corners

Unfortunately these were the very rooms which were remodelled by the 7th Viscount a few years later so we

have no precise idea of what the chimneypieces and their shelf arrangements looked like. However, what may be an early 18th century marble surround was removed from the Bretton Room in 1947 but survives and can be made out in an old photograph of the room when used as an armoury. It has almost identical counterparts in one of the closets at Beningbrough (finished c. 1716), in the room from Clifford's Inn (c. 1686–88) now in the Victoria & Albert Museum and at Rainham, Hanbury and Honington Halls. In 1719, shortly after Beningbrough was complete, John Thorp of Bakewell invoiced Viscount Irwin for four marble chimneypieces, 'In the Gallery not set up . . . my Lady's Dressing Room . . . the Study upstairs', at a total of £24 5s od. It is therefore tempting to associate one of these payments with it. Another has in the past also been associated with Thorp. During alterations in 1945 a chimneypiece loosely conforming to a design in James Gibbs's *Book of Architecture*, 1728, was brought from a room in the stables and set up in what was a small bedroom on the

West Wing. This is now thought to be the marriage of a finely carved satyr mask, perhaps dating from this period, with other elements carved in the 19th century to make it into a chimneypiece. Thorp's chimneypiece destined for the Gallery was indeed set up opposite the two existing fireplaces which were on the north wall, presumably in order to make the room habitable in winter. All three were swept away in the 7th Viscount's alterations twenty years later.

Another housepainter's bill, that of William Addinell, records decoration done at Temple Newsam in 1718. Besides '. . . ye Picture over ye Chimney [in the Hall] Cleaning Mending & Varnish:' he mentions chimneypieces in the steward's dining room, 'my L[ord's] dineing roome Marble' and references to marbling of columns in the Hall, some of which may have belonged to the fireplace rather than to the screen.

The period of ownership of Henry, 7th Viscount Irwin, and his wife Anne, which lasted from 1736 to 1758, saw the most radical and large scale improvements to the house and most of them fortunately still survive. Their architect was almost certainly Daniel Garrett, who succeeded Henry Flitcroft as personal clerk of works and draughtsman to Richard Boyle, 3rd Earl of Burlington, the foremost champion in England of the architecture of Andrea Palladio. This explains why Garrett chose for the magnificent new Saloon, which he converted from the Jacobean Long Gallery, two chimneypieces based on a design by William Kent, published by John Vardy in his *Designs of Inigo Jones and William Kent* in 1735 (Figs 2 and 3). They were set up by the mason Robert Doe and his two men, the work taking 54 days in total. They are executed in plaster (not stone) with wooden overmantels which frame paintings by Antonio Ioli (*c.* 1700–77), an Italian who only arrived in England in 1744. These paintings — a view of Rome on the Tiber, and an architectural fantasy after an engraving by Codazzo — were clearly painted for these positions and must have been amongst his earliest commissions. They are mentioned in an inventory of 1750. The putti that top the overmantels are emblematic of the seasons.

The other major interior of this period is the Library and here the same inventory records a painting of St Francis by Van Dyke, presumably also framed in the overmantel. This ensemble was removed when the Library was converted into a chapel in 1877 but has been identified in a photograph of what had been a dressing room taken between 1922 and *c.* 1940 (Fig. 4). Subsequently the chimneypiece and overmantel were separated, the former set up in a different room, the latter used as the frame to a showcase. The identification of these as being from the Library, Daniel Garrett's most Palladian room at Temple Newsam, is strengthened by the fact that each element derives from a plate in the same publication from which Garrett took the design of the chimneypieces in the Saloon. (The designs were clearly very fashionable in the 1730s for they were engraved by Thomas Langley in 1739 and published by Batty Langley

Fig. 4 *Chimneypiece and overmantel c.1740, probably made for the Library by Richard Fisher of York*

in his *Treasury of Designs* in 1750). Philip Hendy, not realising that the chimneypiece was based on an engraved design, misunderstood its proportions and built it up so that it is now taller than it should be. The 1808 Inventory records 'a plaister Bronze Figure on the chimneypiece', presumably comparatively small and not one of the set of fifteen busts attributed to John Cheere: four of these were in the Library, but probably placed on the cornice; two

Fig. 5   *Chimneypiece c.1740, probably
by Richard Fisher of York*

like Fisher, but it is noticeable that a characteristic ribbon and rosette motif occurs on both chimneypiece and picture frame.

Stylistically of the same date is the plaster chimneypiece shown in early photographs of the Boudoir (Fig. 6) but moved to 'Room VII' ('2nd Room 1st Floor') in the 1940s. However, the Boudoir, from the accounts, seems to have had a marble chimneypiece set up in 1739 (at a cost of 4s 2d and 10d for squaring a marble slab), so this plaster example may just be a Victorian one, of a kind that were widely available then, as has recently been suggested.

The room to the north of the Boudoir had an 18th-century marble surround with a Victorian mantel-shelf on the north wall. These were removed in the 1940s when the oak cabinets were brought up from the Still Room for display purposes, but part of the marble surround was re-used in the Boudoir and there are other fragments which may also belong with it. Could they be the marble chimneypiece for the Chintz room, whose freight cost 9s in 1741?

At either end of the new Saloon, Jacobean window bays on the north side of the house had to be blocked to

seemed to have strayed on to the mantel shelf in the Great Hall (Cat. 68).

The details of the chimneypiece and its overmantel are close enough to the other fine quality mid 18th-century chimneypiece in what is known as the Blue Damask Room (Fig. 5) to suggest that they were the work of the same carver. This was almost certainly the York craftsman Richard Fisher, who was paid the first instalment of a total of £49 in 1740. A simpler version of the latter chimneypiece is in the Sterne Room at Grays Court in York, which centres on a marble portrait medallion of Augusta, wife of Frederick Prince of Wales and mother of George III, whose portrait also appears, in plaster, on the ceiling of the Saloon at Temple Newsam. Details of the doorcases in the Saloon, known to be by Fisher, are identical to doorcases in the Sterne Room in York, so Richard Fisher was presumably responsible for all this work. Fletcher Moss illustrated a photograph in 1910 showing the chimneypiece in the Blue Damask room with the charming full length portrait of Miss Ingram in its spectacular rococo frame forming a 'chimney picture' (Fig. 5). Now stripped, this frame was certainly once painted and might originally have been conceived for this very position. It was clearly the work of a professional frame maker rather than a house-carver

Fig. 6   *Chimneypiece, plaster, 18th or 19th century*

provide flues for various rooms. The Library chimney piece has already been discussed; a chimneypiece was certainly provided in Mrs Clayton's room, in the north-west corner of the building on the ground floor, and this was a bolection moulding. The 'New Bed Chamber' above, and the room over that, must have had new ones too but these are not among the three other rooms recorded in the accounts as being fitted with chimneypieces during the late 1730s: the prices paid were £3, £2, 15s and 10s. Taking together the evidence of the 18th-century bills, early photographs, Philip Hendy's notes written in the 1940s and the two surviving examples still in the house, it seems as if by 1740 there were at least eight bolection moulding chimneypieces, of marble or stone, at Temple Newsam.

One of the last recorded payments was the sum of 4s 2d in March 1739 for 'Setting the Great Hall range' which took three days, probably a new model introduced for greater efficiency. From then on we have to rely on other sources of information: occasionally chimneypieces survive; more rarely old photographs show others now lost. The next structural work in the house was done sometimes after 1767, probably by John Carr. The main staircase was moved from its original position to its present one immediately to the north, involving alterations in the rooms to the west of it. They were reduced in length and their fireplaces were left somewhat awkwardly in a corner, as a pre-war photograph of one shows

Fig. 7 Chimneypiece, late 1760s, probably designed by John Carr

(Fig. 7). Its veined marble and carved wood mouldings were probably Carr's work and it survived until the 1940s when a marble chimneypiece was inserted a few feet further west: Carr's fluted moulding was re-used over a doorway on the north-west stairs.

The need to accommodate her five daughters and their growing families, as well as her wish to provide more fashionable reception rooms on the ground floor, led the widow of the 9th Viscount to commission a Leeds architect, William Johnson, to remodel the whole of the south wing. Most of the work was completed between 1792 and 1796; in 1808 two lumber rooms in the south-east corner of the house had evidently not yet been converted and their contents included 'an old marble chimney piece and hearth [a] new statuary chimney piece and carved blocks and 2 veined marble hearths'. Although these late 18th-century rooms survive, only one, the Great Hall, has its contemporary chimneypiece. This is a handsome stone example in neoclassical taste, now painted white. In 1808 there were, on the shelf, '2 white painted plaister heads . . . a wedgewood Vase'. Early photographs show it with a dark, grained finish, applied strapwork decoration, made of lead, and surmounted by a richly carved Jacobean-style overmantel (Fig. 8). These features, which were removed in the 1940s, are now thought to belong to the substantial redecoration of much of the house done for Lady Hertford in 1827–28. This is only recorded in an extract from the letter book of Elizabeth Gott for 3 May 1828: '. . . they are now furnishing and painting the house, the gallery and lower rooms were done last year & are very handsome & comfortable . . .'. The substantial built-in register grate of distinctly Regency character, visible in the photographs, confirms this date. A photograph taken early this century shows it with a complete set of furniture: these include a six-piece garniture of Chinese porcelain, an elaborate fender, a pair of pole screens and a cheval fire-screen, a dummy-board figure and a hearth rug. Either side of the chimneypieces is its attendant lighting equipment, two-light lamps on tall, elaborately carved stands.

Beyond the Great Hall is Lady Hertford's most celebrated interior, the Chinese Drawing Room, hung with a hand-painted Chinese wallpaper 'improved' by the addition of some birds cut from Audubon's *Birds of America*. Again, a pre-war photograph shows a handsome Regency grate contained within a chaste, white marble chimneypiece with sunk tablet and panels, surmounted by a Louis XV style overmantel glass (Fig. 9). Regrettably all these features were removed in 1939 when the room was refurnished, an unworthy Louis XVI-style wooden chimneypiece of mean proportions being brought in and painted to match the room decoration. Philip Hendy, who introduced these alterations, considered that the marble chimneypiece he removed dated from 1796.

At the other end of the Great Hall, the New Terrace Room (as it was called in the 1808 inventory of goods belonging to Lady Hertford's mother) has suffered equally badly. Lady Hertford panelled it in oak and composition probably to take a series of Beauvais tapestries, but everything was removed at the sale of Temple Newsam in 1922. The white marble chimneypiece, either of 1796 or 1827–28, was described in 1944 as 'plain' and was replaced by a more ornate specimen which, ostensibly of late 18th-century date, is a modern amalgam of elements from several different chimneypieces.

The Dining Room in the south-west corner of the house, and the two rooms north of it, were also probably remodelled by Lady Hertford. Until the 1890s, as shown on an old floor-plan, the Dining Room clearly had a classical chimneypiece, dating either from the second half of the 18th century or from the Regency. It is possible,

Fig. 9 *Chimneypiece and grate, made for the Chinese Drawing Room in 1827–28*

Fig. 8 *Chimneypiece of c.1796 and overmantel perhaps of 1827–28 in the Great Hall*

therefore, that the handsome stone chimneypiece with its Regency-style grate which survives in a ground floor room in the Stable Block came from the Dining Room when C. E. Kempe remodelled it in the 1890s (Fig. 10). The '5 pieces of Wedgewood ware' mentioned here in 1808 were presumably arranged on the chimneypiece. The room next door has lost its chimneypiece but in the one beyond there is still a Regency example made of a red marble streaked with white.

Upstairs the losses are more severe: not one of the late Georgian or Regency fireplaces survives. The Prince's Room in the south east corner of the house had, perhaps only from 1868 when it was occupied by the Prince of Wales (later Edward VII), a carved oak chimneypiece which seems to have survived a chimney fire in the 1890s until it was supplanted by a white marble Regency period chimneypiece brought from Methley Hall in 1957. In the South Bedroom is a bolection-mould chimneypiece with shelf, made of Derbyshire marble with a carved leaf in white marble forming a pseudo-keystone. The arched

Fig. 10 Regency grate perhaps displaced from the Dining Room in the 1890s

grate is original to it and the whole ensemble must date from 1868. The next three rooms lost their fireplaces in order to make space for the paintings from the City Art Gallery in 1939, while that in the French Room was revealed again in 1983: it probably dates from the end of the 19th century as do most of the indigenous grates still remaining in the house: considerations of economy probably dictated that as soon as the German steam-type central heating system was installed in the 1890s the size of the firegrates should be reduced to the bare minimum.

The so-called Darnley Room has had a particularly complex history of redecoration. Part of Sir Arthur Ingram's Jacobean additions, this was the room that had marbled decoration on the chimney breast. It was remodelled in the later 17th century and hung with damask, later replaced by wallpaper, but in the 1890s Mrs Meynell Ingram evoked, as in her staircase, the Jacobean era by panelling the room once more, replicating a plaster frieze and ceiling, and installing a heavy carved oak chimneypiece which framed a 17th-or 18th-century bolection-mould fire surround. Several early photographs indicate even the garniture which consisted of five somewhat ill-assorted pieces of china with a candlestick either end, or seven pieces, with lighting provided by brass wall-sconces. In 1957 an imposing Istria marble chimneypiece of Italianate character probably supplied by Gillows of Lancaster for Bridge House, Bury, Lancashire about 1910, was installed.

Mrs Meynell Ingram spent much of her time at the other end of the house, her bedroom being what had in 1808 been Lady Irwin's Dressing Room: it then had at least 'fifteen pieces of different sorts of China figures and vases on the Chimney piece'. A late 19th-century photograph shows a handsome chimney piece of statuary and Siena marbles with detached Ionic columns. This may date from the Regency or as late as the 1860s. Described as 'ugly' in 1947 it was removed, the dado being continued across the void, and in 1948 a rococo

carved pine chimneypiece from Darrington Hall, Essex, was set up instead. The marble one survives in fragmentary state and will be reinstated in due course.

In the 1890s Mrs Meynell Ingram employed the architect, C. E. Kempe, to remodel the Dining Room. He took his cue from the Jacobean ceiling and frieze which had miraculously survived from Sir Arthur Ingram's time (perhaps Lady Hertford in her 1827–28 alterations had respected the existing character of the room), and installed a magnificent chimneypiece based on the one in the hall at Hardwick — an archaeological touch typical of his work at Temple Newsam. The arms and motto of Henry Lord Darnley combine with those of the Ingrams to reinforce the distinguished history of the house. Very little has altered since then, except that some large figured tiles have been removed from the fire-opening. Sometime during the 19th century simple stone fireplaces with chamfered details were inserted into the corners of four servants' bedrooms in the part of the house called Smithfield, above the Saloon.

Many of the changes made during the present century have already been referred to and there is little more that needs recording. In 1912 Lenygons were commissioned to alter the room at the end of the ground floor of the South wing from a billiard room to a Library. The handsome chimneypiece of white marble streaked with grey surmounted by carved wood originally painted green and gilded was designed by Ralph Freeman-Smith. This is very similar in character to the well-known chimneypiece in the Parlour at Rousham in Oxfordshire, designed by William Kent and carved by John Marden between 1738 and 1740. It may be that an exact parallel exists elsewhere. The historical accuracy of Freeman-Smith's design may be explained by the fact that Francis Lenygon, that avid researcher of the decorative arts in England, was connected with the firm. The scheme here included a built-in register grate and a pair of carved swags on the chimney-breast. Amongst the all-too numerous changes made in the 1930s and '40s was the insertion into the Green Damask Room of a fine quality rococo-style carved pine chimneypiece brought from Seacroft Hall in 1938, which was at first stripped but was subsequently painted in with the room. According to Philip Hendy, this replaced a white marble chimneypiece probably of Victorian date, while the original one of the mid 18th century was apparently a bolection moulding, later removed to the Steward's room and sold to Pratts in 1944 in part exchange for the one set up in the Terrace Room.

If the story outlined here emphasizes an astonishingly cavalier attitude towards what one might have thought relatively permanent features of a historic house, we are fortunate that so many clues remain to make the job of reparation possible. The removal of decorative wallpapers (many now triumphantly reprinted and rehung) did much to destroy the atmosphere of the rooms: the obliteration of their chimneypieces took away their life. So these are now to be reinstated wherever possible.

A CHECKLIST OF CHIMNEYPIECES
AT TEMPLE NEWSAM IN 1984

The numbers in brackets are those used in the Perspective Floor Plan in the current guidebook.

GREAT HALL (1): 1796, stone now white painted. The Regency grate, applied decoration and overmantel were removed in the 1940s

SOUTH-EAST ROOM (2): 1912, marble and wood, designed by Ralph Freeman-Smith of Lenygons

CHINESE DRAWING ROOM (3): Louis XVI style, bought in Harrogate 1939. Replaced Regency chimneypiece and grate installed in 1827–28 (Fig. 9)

NEW TERRACE ROOM (4): neoclassical style, acquired 1944, replacing a white marble one either of 1796 or 1827

DINING ROOM: 1890s, designed by C. E. Kempe. A Regency chimneypiece and grate now in a ground floor room in the Stable block may formerly have been here (Fig. 10)

1ST ROOM 1ST FLOOR (6): early Georgian style and said to have come from a room in the Stables but probably a composite piece. Set up 1944–45 replacing a chimneypiece probably designed by John Carr, with a 19th-century grate (Fig. 7)

2ND ROOM 1ST FLOOR (7): 18th century or later, plaster, (Fig. 6) moved from the Boudoir (10) in 1944–45. The former chimneypiece (now in the Boudoir) had an overmantel frame, and together (Fig. 4) they were probably made for the Library c. 1745 where they remained until 1877

BLUE DAMASK ROOM (8): 1740s, carved pine, probably by Richard Fisher of York and original to the mid 18th-century alterations (Fig. 5). Tudor fire arch behind damask wallcovering

GREEN DAMASK ROOM (9): 1760s, from Seacroft Hall 1938. Replaced a white marble chimneypiece said to be Victorian, the mid 18th century original probably being a marble bolection moulding part-exchanged in 1944

BOUDOIR (10): 1740s (Fig. 4), moved here from Room 7 in 1944–45 but originally in the Library

NORTH-WEST ROOM (12): mid 18th-century, ex Darrington Hall, Essex 1947. Replaced a Regency or later 19th-century white and Siena marble chimneypiece which survives in part in the cellars

SALOON (13): 1740, plaster and pine, by Robert Doe, after a design by William Kent published by John Vardy in 1735 (Figs 2 and 3)

LIBRARY (14): in the 1740s the chimneypiece in Room 10 and overmantel in Room 7 were probably here (Fig. 4)

PRINCE'S ROOM (17): Regency, ex Methley Hall 1957. Replaced a carved oak chimneypiece possibly of 1868

SOUTH BEDROOM (18): fossiliferous and statuary marble; contemporary grate, possibly 1868

LADY WILLIAM GORDON'S ROOM (22): c. 1900, white marble; contemporary grate

DARNLEY ROOM (23): c. 1910, made by Gillows for Bridge House, Bury, Lancashire. Set up here in 1957, replacing carved oak chimneypiece of the 1890s

In addition, a red marble chimneypiece veined with white still exists in a ground floor room; two bolection mouldings and two plaster chimneypieces, together with four stop-chamfered stone chimneypieces, survive in other rooms. Several further chimneypieces were removed in a fragmentary state to the cellars in the 1940s and 50s.

FIRE FURNITURE

Inventories contain valuable if tantalizing information about interiors. The Ham House inventories of 1677, 1679 and 1683 (reprinted in *Furniture History*, 1980) are particularly rewarding because so many of the items listed survive. The principal apartments were equipped with sets of silver garnished hearth furniture usually comprising an ornamental cast-iron fireback, a pair of andirons or a fire pan, a shovel, tongs, bellows, broom and either a silver hearth rod or a gilt brass fender. The implements in the best rooms were suspended from silver hooks. These luxurious articles seem to have been supplied about 1675. The Hall was provided with a 'great Iron grate' which, to judge from the presence of a fire shovel, tongs and fork was used for burning logs and/or coal. This survives, it is a large rectangular basket with the front bars divided by a central stanchion, and give a clue to the character of the 'large double grate' recorded in the Hall and elsewhere at Dyrham in 1710.

The Dyrham inventory nicely documents the period of transition from burning logs supported on the hearth-stone by andirons and the introduction of coal fired grates. It is also noteworthy for the numerous references to 'A Delf Flower pot in ye Chimney' or 'A Large Pyramid Delf Flower pot in ye Chimney' — many of these spectacular vases are preserved at the house. There is also one pleasing allusion to a dummy-board figure in the Ante-Hall 'A Woman pareing of an Apple' — they were once thought of as chimney accessories, but are now believed to be whimisical eye-catchers placed at random in a room.

Many of the lesser apartments at Dyrham were provided only with a pair of andirons, sometimes accompanied by a 'fire pan' for holding burning charcoal when a log fire was not required. A 'Wood Grate' often associated with 'a pr of brass Dogs' recorded in several rooms probably represents the compiler's attempt to describe a basket grate resting on the billet bars of andirons. Other chambers such as the Family Parlour contained stove grates for coal together with a fender, fire shovel, tongs, poker, brush and perhaps a pair of bellows, whereas the wood burning grates only required tongs and a hearth brush. The 1742 Dyrham inventory still lists many delft pots standing in the fireplaces, dogs were retained in a few rooms, there is a reference to a chimney board and the kitchen chamber contained '2 forrest grates' — a term applied to hob grates which provided two flat surfaces level with the top fire bar for boiling kettles.

The 1727 inventory of Kiveton, Derbyshire, a palatial, luxuriously furnished country house built by the Duke of Leeds in 1705 contains a detailed record of chimney furniture. As at Dyrham individual hearths were equipped for burning either wood or coal, in fact old fashioned log fires seem to have been preferred in some important state apartments — evidently a traditional blaze was, even in 1727, a welcome sight in rooms such as the Great Drawing Room which contained:

1 Iron Cast Back

1 pr of Large Andirons Brass & Silver'd

1 Less pair for Doggs Do

Shovel & Tongs with Knobs Silver'd

Bellows & Hearth Broom

2 Steel pins

The latter may have been crooks flanking the chimney-piece to prop fire irons upright such as can still be seen in the Hall at Ham House. The Drawing Room and Dining Room contained modern grates with fenders and fire irons, while other interiors were provided with brass or steel 'wind stow grates' which had cast backs and the usual complement of coal burning implements. Eleven chimney boards were stored in a coal closet.

The inventories of Appuldurcombe Park (1780) and Harewood (1795) — both neoclassical show houses — illustrate various points. At the former the Dining Parlour boasted 'A Steel grate with compass front and therm feet fluted & engraved, a fender to match, a pair of tongs, shovel and poker'. Most of the bedrooms contained, as was usual at this date, ordinary bath grates except for Sir Richard and Lady Worsley's which had 'A Stove (in the manner of Brodie)'. It is noteworthy that by 1780 bellows are absent, hearth brushes or brooms are seldom mentioned, wire fenders start to appear and there is still no sign of coal scuttles in fashionable rooms. The Harewood inventory records numerous green fenders (having a brass frame and painted lattice grilles), also several hearth rooks — a type of key for adjusting register grates.

Although Temple Newsam was furnished over several generations it is likely that many of the hearths were re-equipped about 1796–1800. A feature of the 1808 inventory is the excessive pains taken to prevent accidental fires. The best dining room was typical in having 'a high polished steel fender' to match the register stove, a fire guard which probably hooked on to the top grate bar, and 'a high painted green wire fender'. The family favoured japanned hearth brooms and 'hearth rug brooms' and Miss Gordon's room apparently contained a companion or stand for fire irons 'a shovel, tongs, poker, hearth broom and stand'.

The Parlington inventory of 1843 confirms that coal boxes had by then become standard requisites and suggests that bellows and brooms were once again in fashion. In most of these inventories the housekeeper's room alone contained cosy domestic paraphernalia such as footmen, trivets and muffin toasters more usually associated with farmhouse kitchens.

FIRE GRATES

In medieval houses fires were commonly built in the centre of the hall, the smoke escaping through a lantern in the roof — evidence of this traditional arrangement can still be seen at Penshurst, Kent and Gainsborough Old Hall, Lincolnshire. Later, chimneys were constructed in the walls and the hearth was provided with andirons to support the billets of wood and sometimes a smaller pair of 'creepers' to prop up partly burned logs. During the Tudor period when 'sea coal' was first used basket grates were introduced to hold the lumps of fuel in a compact mass — thus the age of the 'raised hearth' began.

For many generations handsome andirons (Cats 1 and 2) remained a conspicuous feature of well furnished hearths, but it is not easy to say whether their presence was merely ceremonial or if they indicate that either coal or log fires could be made up. However, some early basket grates were supported on the billet bars of andirons and occasionally andirons are found with hooks behind the uprights for holding removable fire bars. These transitional grates suggest that innovations to such a time-honoured spectacle were slow to gain acceptance.

The 'great Iron grate' recorded in the Hall at Ham House in the 1670s is likely to be the large rectangular double-fronted one which survives *in situ* and to judge from the assortment of implements it was used for burning either logs and/or coal. The family rooms at Ham and Knole at this date were provided with fire pans for holding burning charcoal. (Cats 3 and 4). This form of heating was probably not very effective since fire pans soon passed out of fashion.

Few Palladian grates have been identified, but the main line of development is reasonably clear. The free-standing rectangular basket was backed by a plain cast-iron plate or fireback resting on wrought iron struts, the sides were also of cast iron and a grid through which loose ash fell formed the bottom. Sometimes removable iron cheeks were fitted at each side to reduce the capacity of the basket (Cats 5, 8, 10 and 15). Decoration was confined to the front, composed of three fire bars and usually a fretted apron with wings ending in ornamental standards which supported the breast. This type was usually called a stove grate in the 18th century.

From about 1750 the design of stove grates became increasingly elaborate, often embodying gothic, rococo or chinoiserie styles. Pattern books issued by cabinetmakers often included a few fashionable examples while J. & W. Welldon (1765) and William Glossop (1771), both smiths by trade, published collections of designs (Figs 15–55). Disappointingly few rococo specimens have been recorded, but many splendid neoclassical grates remain particularly in Robert Adam's interiors (Cats 6, 7, 8 and 10); those at Kedleston are particularly ambitious. The hob grate which was to become widely popular may have first appeared in the domestic offices of country houses about 1720. They

were built into the fireplace opening, the fire bars being set between two cast-iron plates capped by hobs on which a kettle could be placed. Hob grates were of three main types termed Bath (Cat. 11), Forest (Cats 12 and 13) or Pantheon according to the shape of the front. There were also local versions such as the Duck's Nest or Sussex hob grate, known as a fore face in Scotland. Late 18th century models may bear the name 'CARRON' or 'C. DALE' —the two leading provincial foundries who mass produced cast-iron wares. The use of moulds tended to encourage conservatism, the same patterns being used for decades and even Edwardian reproductions (Cat. 11).

Following the introduction of stove grates the size of fireplace openings was reduced to concentrate the up-draught, so paving the way for the framed or enclosed grate. If the air current was too strong, the fire consumed vast quantities of coal and all the heat went up the chimney; if on the other hand it was sluggish the smoke billowed back into the room. An attempt at fine adjustment of the opening was the register grate which occupied the entire fireplace and was fitted with a movable iron plate in the flue to regulate the up-draught (Fig. 11). This type of grate was first widely used during the third quarter of the 18th century and although not particularly efficient in terms of fuel consumption it went a long way towards solving smoke nuisance and with various refinements continued in production throughout the next century. There is a particularly decorative polished steel register grate of 1786 in the State Bed Room (now the south library) at Audley End enriched with red and blue enamel jewel work in the engraved decoration which was probably intended to harmonize

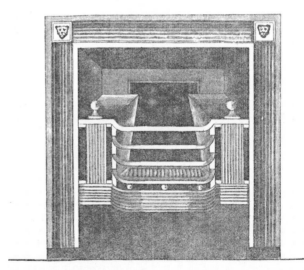

Fig. 11 M & G Skidmore, 1811, pl.25. 'A Convex Reed Elliptic Register Stove, with Bright framed Fire, Double Rail, Balls, Bright Heads, Bevil Cheeks, falling Back, and Valve.'

with the embroidered state bed by Chipchase & Co, still in the collection.

The Welldons' *Smith's Right Hand*, 1765, contained eighteen designs for Venetian or Philadelphia stoves, types which are now exceedingly rare, two of the few extant examples surviving at Ston Easton Park, Somerset and Buxted Park, Sussex. These consisted of splendidly elaborate cast-iron fireplace surrounds fitted with an integral grate and offered uninhibited scope for displays of ornament. The trade names suggest they were inspired by foreign models and may have been intended for export.

The American soldier, statesman and inventor Count Rumford published, in 1797, an influential essay on the design of grates; his specifications were widely applied and the term 'Rumford grate' frequently occurs during the early 19th century. He solved the problem of smoky chimneys and excessive fuel consumption by contracting the opening and lowering the grate. By advancing the back, splaying the sides and constructing the fireplace of brick rather than iron, he dramatically improved their heat reflecting qualities. Rumford appreciated that radiant heat was more effective than hot air for warming rooms.

Various metals were used for grates. In the early-Georgian period they were usually of cast-iron with steel fire bars. Brass or bell metal might be employed for embellishments such as ornamental finials, a pierced apron, the fender and fire irons, a few hob grates constructed of cast brass are known. Fine brass register grates were made by Dublin ironmongers, of whom two at least inscribed their names on the front. At Castle Coole there are two, one signed 'George Binns / Dame Street' (Fig. 12) the other lettered 'GEO:E BINNS DAME | ST DUBLIN'. The surrounds are engraved in the neoclassical taste. Similar grates bearing the name 'J and ? Clarke' exist at Derrymore House, near Newry and Townley Hall, Drogheda (information from Peter Marlow).

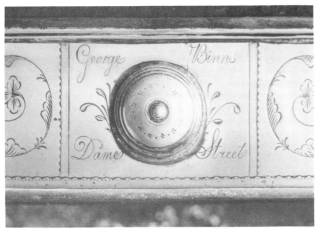

Fig. 12 Detail of brass register grate, c.1780 by George Binns, Dame Street, Dublin, from Castle Coole, Ireland.

National Trust

Towards the middle of the 18th century brightly polished steel which possessed a gleaming silvery sheen became the standard material for smart free-standing stove grates, still of course with a cast-iron fireback. However, an even more luxurious silvery metal called paktong was favoured by Robert Adam when his clients could afford it. Paktong was an alloy of copper, zinc and nickle imported from China, the name deriving from the local word pai-tung meaning white copper. It was hard, easily cast, did not tarnish, could be readily engraved and polished and possessed a beautiful lustrous sheen. In Europe it was sometimes erroneously termed Tutenag — another silvery oriental alloy. It is not known who actually manufactured the impressive paktong stove grates ordered for Syon, Saltram, Croome Court, Osterley, Battle Abbey and elsewhere, they were presumably produced by leading London smiths. A magnificent suite of paktong chimney furniture designed by Robert Adam (Cat. 9) for the Drawing Room at Osterley (Cat. 8) is particularly rare, being invested with a golden hue, presumably to match the gilt furniture in the room. Towards the end of the century supplies of this splendid metal seem to have ceased.

The Regency period saw a return to favour of rectangular cast-iron grates, often with brass or bright steel mouldings and applied ornaments. Jutsham's day book (pp. 70–71) describes handsome specimens and names the suppliers. Improved casting techniques allowed greater definition and sharpness in the decorative details and with the gathering pace of the industrial revolution increased emphasis was placed on devising improved models. During the Victorian period profuse ornamental elaboration ruled.

The following notes which could easily be multiplied draw attention to signed or documented grates at a few country houses open to the public. At Kenwood, Hampstead, the grates date from various periods. None were designed by Robert Adam, although the Soane Museum drawings include his designs for a chimney board, the Chinese fireplace in the Upper Hall and other chimneypieces in the house. In the 1790s new polished steel grates were installed in the Library and Dining Room, the former with patent ventilation system by 'OLDHAM LONDON'. In 1787 James Oldham also supplied stoves and fenders for the Great Hall at Carlton House (PRO. HO 73/32). Several new cast-iron grates were fitted in 1816, including an X-frame hob grate in the Breakfast Room and a 'Pantheon' in the entrance Hall.

Much has been lost at Marble Hill, Twickenham but the house still contains three original decorative cast-iron Burton grates in the Wrought Room, Great Room and Dining Room, (the latter inscribed on the back 'PUBLISHED BY BURTON & Co | LONDON FEBRUARY 5th 1810 BLOOMSBURY'. Another Burton grate (dated 1811) was recently purchased and in 1981 a Carron grate of c. 1824 was bought.

Two grates at Heaton Hall, Manchester, are documented by entries in Lord Wilton's cash book (information from James Lomax). The one in the Dining Room was supplied by Horsley in 1775 at a cost of £25 (possibly Horsley & Scott, brass founders, recorded in Habadashers Walk, Hoxton, in that year). In 1790 Brodie and Young, iron founders, Glass House Yard, Blackfriars, provided the Music Room grate for £41 14s 0d. References to Brodie grates are fairly numerous, they are mentioned in the Appuldurcombe inventory of 1780 and Christie's sale, no. 38 (1781) lists '10 Register Stoves of Brodie's patent'. The bath stove and two stand grates ordered for Heaton in 1774 from Henry Tobin of Leeds have not survived.

Cast-iron Gothic grates, fire backs and wrought iron/brass andirons in the Long Gallery, Drawing Room and private apartments at Chirk Castle, North Wales were made by Hardmans of Birmingham after designs by A. W. Pugin in 1846–47. The owner, Col Robert Myddleton Biddulph, complained of their highly uneconomical design which he considered wasteful of fuel. Pugin wrote despairingly to J. G. Crace 'I could make a church as easy as a grate. Such a job as Chirk is enough to drive any man mad. All little things are as difficult to get properly done as the greatest. It is worse than the House of Lords' (information from Richard Dean quoting RIBA, MS, PUG 3/20). At Penrhyn Castle, also in North Wales, all the massive neo-Norman chimney furniture is attributable to the architect Thomas Hopper, and dates from the 1820s and 30s. At Plas Newydd, Anglesea, the steel fire grates in the Octagon Room, Saloon and various other apartments are believed to have been supplied by Dearman and Francis of Birmingham during the alterations of the 1790s.

Although strictly falling outside the time frame of this survey the fine collection of mid-Victorian cast-iron firegrates at Norwich Museum by Barnard, Bishops & Barnards of Norfolk ironworks, Norwich after designs by Thomas Jeckyll deserve a passing mention.

1 Pair of andirons
c. 1675
Iron and silver
Iron billet bars with standards, each headed by a demi-putto emerging from an acanthus skirt with one upraised arm
h. 22, l. 34

'Doggs garnished with silver' are mentioned on several hearths in the Ham inventories of 1677, 1679 and 1683

Lent by the Trustees of the Victoria & Albert Museum (Ham House)

2 Pair of andirons
17th century, last quarter
Brass and iron
The billet bars and concealed inner stems are of iron; the gadrooned vase-shaped standards enriched with acanthus headed by cup and cover finials are raised on plinths supported by scroll feet faced with putto masks. There are many magnificent sets of ornate andirons at Knole including several luxurious silver pairs
h. 68, w. 34, d. 47

Lent by the National Trust (Knole)

3 Fire pan
c. 1675
Iron and silver
The rectangular tray with cable twist border is framed by a cushion moulded surround which is overlaid by an openwork system of acanthus fronds executed in embossed and chased silver; the front centres on a silver-gilt cypher J L E D beneath a Ducal coronet. The pan is supported on two lions couchant in cast sliver. Side lifting handles missing
w. 54, d. 38

Made for John and Elizabeth (neé Dysart) Lauderdale who married in 1672, he was created Duke later the same year. Silver mounted fire pans are recorded in several rooms in the Ham House inventories of 1677, 1679 and 1683

Lent by the Trustees of the Victoria & Albert Museum (Ham House)

4 Fire pan
17th century, second half
Brass and iron
Of horse-shoe design, the trough is made of sheet brass with an iron bottom and splayed back. The cabriole forelegs with paw feet and shells on the knees and the scroll handles are of brass. Fire pans held burning charcoal
h. 34, w. 55, d. 42

Lent by the National Trust (Knole)

5 Double stove grate
Mid-18th century
Cast-iron
Rectangular with column standards headed by wrythen
flame finials, the basket is fitted with loose wedge-shaped
iron cheeks
h. 84, w. 106
Formerly at Methley Hall, Yorkshire

Leeds City Art Galleries (Temple Newsam)

6 Stove grate
Maurice Tobin, Leeds, c. 1770
Bright steel
Inscribed: '[MAU]RICE T[OBIN] | [LE]EDS'
A handsome, provenanced grate by a known maker; the
pierced apron still betrays rococo impulses
w. 91

Lent by Mr and Mrs Robin Compton (Newby Hall)

7 Double stove grate
Tobin, Leeds, c. 1773
Bright steel
Inscribed: 'TOBIN LEEDS | 1522'
This splendid grate was commissioned for the Tapestry
Room designed by Adam and furnished by Chippendale,
it is one of the most sumptuous and complete of all
neoclassical English country house interiors. The
matching fender (Cat. 18) is signed by Rodgers who took
over Tobin's business in 1773/74. The fire irons which
presumably had wrythen flame terminals to match the
finials have not survived, but a set from Harewood,
attributed to Tobin, displays this feature (Cat. 30).
Pattern numbers are sometimes quoted in Tobin's
Harewood account
w. 103

Lent by Mr and Mrs Robin Compton (Newby Hall)

8 Stove grate and fender
Designed by Robert Adam, c. 1773
Paktong
Recorded in the 1782 Osterley inventory (Drawing
Room) 'A very Elegant Tutenage Stove a ditto fender
shovel tongs and poker with tutenage Vase nobs' The fire
irons and Adam's design are catalogued under Nos 9
and 31
The grate has a plain inner structure of cast iron with an
elaborate paktong frontispiece, the golden hue of which

harmonizes with the gilt furniture in the room. The fire basket contains two splayed cast-iron cheeks. There are minor differences between Adam's drawing and the executed design. For instance the two standing figures (taken from his design for part of the pier commodes) are replaced by a classical medallion head, the cresting ornament was omitted, the vases simplified and the number of motifs in the running pattern on the apron and fender varied. The cast double serpentine breakfront fender styled to match the apron on the grate has a steel lining and shoe. The anthemion motif is repeated on the frieze of the room, the double acanthus scroll occurs on the chimneypiece and other details relate to the pier commodes

Grate l. 115, fender l. 142

Lent by the Trustees of the Victoria & Albert Museum (Osterley Park)

Shovle tongs and pokers'. The fire irons with knobs matching the finials on the grate are catalogued under No. 33

The grate has a plain inner structure of cast-iron with an elaborate bright steel frontispiece the apron of which is styled to match the fender. The square tapered standards with husk loops and leaf-cup toes correspond to the legs of the library table and set of chairs probably made by John Linnell who is also known to have designed stove grates. The engraved openwork pattern of strapwork with alternating florets and husk motifs matches the straight fender and is closely related to the carved frieze on the library chimneypieces. The fire basket contains two hollow cast-iron cheeks

Grate l. 94, fender l. 148

Lent by the Trustees of the Victoria & Albert Museum (Osterley Park)

8

9

9 Drawing for a stove grate and fender
Robert Adam, c. 1773
Pen and grey wash, 47 × 34
Inscribed: 'Design for a Grate for the Drawing Room at Osterley', with a scale at the bottom. The minor but significant differences between this drawing and the grate as executed are noted under Cat. 8. They show how Adam tended to include decorative elements which looked fine on the drawing board but needed to be modified or omitted when translated by a tradesman

Lent by the Trustees of the Victoria & Albert Museum (Osterley Park)

10 Stove grate and fender (one of a pair)
c. 1775
Iron and polished steel
Recorded in the 1782 Osterley inventory (Library): 'Two handsome and engraved Steel Stoves two ditto fenders

11 Bath stove grate
Possibly by Carron Co., Scotland, 18th century, last quarter
Cast-iron with brass apron
The side panels centre on oval medallions suspended from tied ribbons enclosing reliefs of classical muses, the cheeks are ornamented with small figures of a musician and a soldier
h. 54, w. 80

Bath grates were often installed in bedrooms. Edwardian copies of this pattern were produced by Carron Co. and Thomas Elsley, Ltd, London

Leeds City Art Galleries (Temple Newsam)

12 Forest hob grate
The Coalbrook Dale Company, after 1781
Cast-iron. Back plate and grille missing; inscribed in raised letters: 'C. Dale' (twice).

10

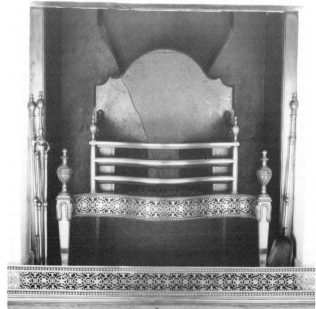

11

12

It is interesting to find the Coalbrook Dale Co. using an image of the famous iron bridge, opened in 1781 to promote their wares. The scrolls above the bridge are inscribed: 'PLAN OF THE IRON BRIDGE|AT COALBROOK-DALE', the words are taken from the plan which accompanied William Ellis' well known engraving of the bridge after Rooker, published in 1781. The Company's great rival Carron produced a very similar hob grate bearing the legend: 'A VIEW OF THE CAST IRON | BRIDGE OVER THE SEVERN'. Several specimens of each type have been recorded, there are three in the museum collection, one of which came from Attingham Park, near Shrewsbury. They are discussed by Stuart Smith, 'The Iron Bridge Fireplace', *Design History Society Newsletter*, April 1983, pp. 25–26
h. 61, w. 70

Lent by the Ironbridge Gorge Museum Trust

13

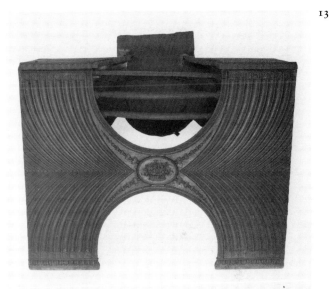

13 Forest hob grate

Carron Co., Scotland, late 18th century
The front plate which centres on a medallion enclosing a basket of flowers is decorated with an overall feather pattern of shallow flutes with formalised leaf borders.
Lettered on left-hand plinth 'CARRON' and on the right 'B'
Bottom bar missing
h. 60, w. 77

Lent by Robert Aagaard

14 Hob grate

Late 18th century
Cast-iron
The front panels centre on oval medallions: the one on the left features a seated lady representing Vigilence, she wears classical robes, holds a bird and is accompanied by a crane, that on the right portrays Hebe with the eagle
h. 60, w. 106

There are hob grates (with cheeks) of identical pattern at Newby Hall, Grimston Hall and another small version at

14

Constable Burton Hall all in Yorkshire. This example came from a house in the Leeds area

Leeds City Art Galleries (Temple Newsam)

15 Grate, andirons and fender
c. 1825
Cast-iron, painted black
The fire back and andirons are decorated with the Holte arms while the fender centres on a tablet bearing the family crest — a squirrel; the grate has loose cheeks at each end. Several unsigned drawings for closely similar heraldic grates survive amongst a large collection of manuscript designs datable to the 1820s associated with Richard Bridgens' work for James Watt at Aston Hall. They are described by Virginia Glenn in *Furniture History,* XV (1979), pp. 54–67
Fender l. 166, andirons h. 107, grate h. 98, w. 85

Lent by Birmingham Museums and Art Gallery (Aston Hall)

15

FENDERS AND GUARDS

Before the period of the raised hearth, and for a while after the appearance of coal burning grates, the floorboards were protected from sparks and falling logs by wide hearth stones which were sometimes made of expensive marble. However, after the Restoration fenders were gradually introduced to provide additional protection. The 1679 Ham inventory yields several references to 'one silver rod upon the hearth' and several still survive: they were decorative moulded strips that cross the hearthstone on a line with the fireplace opening and served only for display. The Green Closet contained a gilt brass fender which is ornamented with a running pattern of pierced acanthus echoing the chimney surround. The Dyrham (1710) and Kiveton (1727) inventories illustrate the increasing usage of fenders. Descriptions are bare and few survive from the early-Georgian period, but the evidence suggests that brass and bell metal fenders were popular.

By the middle of the 18th century polished or 'bright' steel grates and fenders had become fashionable. These are often finely pierced and engraved to match the fretwork aprons of grates and designs appeared in metal work and furniture pattern books. Robert Adam, who was always at pains to create unified schemes designed magnificent grates *en suite* with fenders that exactly fitted the fireplace aperture (Cat. 9). In some of his most luxurious interiors at Osterley, Saltram and Syon the fenders were made of paktong (Cat. 8). About 1750 metal bottom plates or 'shoes' as they were called were introduced to protect the now much smaller hearth-stones. The early 19th century saw a return to favour of brass fenders usually with rounded corners, raised on ball or lion paw feet and fitted with standards at each end headed by crooks to support the fire irons (Cat. 21). About 1815 decorative cast-iron fenders were first made, they sometimes incorporated low implement rests bedded onto the shoe. The earliest Carron Co. catalogue, (SRO GD 85/15/5) illustrates extensions which could be attached to the top rail of fenders to increase their height.

The Regency period was the age of very impressive hearth furniture in wealthy households. Many spectacularly embellished examples are listed under the names of suppliers in Jutsham's day book recording the arrival and despatch of furnishings at Carlton House between 1806 and 1829 (see pp. 70–71). There are at Heaton Hall, Manchester two particularly fine bright steel fenders inlaid with brass which relate to rare copies of drawings by George Bullock at Birmingham Art Gallery (Cat. 22). Another handsome steel and brass example from Newby is shown as Cat. 20.

Fireguards differ from fenders in being utility articles. They were of two kinds, both constructed of wire latticework; the smaller variety was intended to hook over the top fire bar and served as a spark guard (Cat. No. 23) whereas the larger form might be up to 3 ft high with brass mouldings and when in position completely enclosed the hearth making it safe. Nicklin & Son of Birmingham were specialist makers. Some were built with folding ends for easy storage, others are of semi-circular design; the wire mesh was often painted green (Cat. 19).

16

17

16 Fender
c. 1770
Brass, with an iron shoe
The openwork design of scrolled foliage centres on a shell flanked by dragons
l. 107

Lent by Mr and Mrs Robin Compton (Newby Hall)

17 Fender
John Rodgers, Leeds, c. 1774
Bright steel, with an iron shoe
Inscribed: 'RODGERS|LEEDS'
A fine fender illustrating the decorative possibilities of combining fretted patterns
l. 158

Lent by Mr and Mrs Robin Compton (Newby Hall)

RODGERS
LEEDS

18

18 Fender
John Rodgers, Leeds, *c.* 1774
Bright steel with an iron shoe
Inscribed: 'RODGERS|LEEDS'
Rodgers took over Tobin's business in 1773–74
Signed fenders are very rare, this finely pierced and
engraved example is *en suite* with the stove grate which
Tobin made for the Tapestry Room (Cat. 7)
l. 150

Lent by Mr and Mrs Robin Compton (Newby Hall)

19

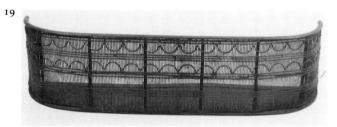

19 Wire fender
Late 18th century
The wire-work grille is supported on eight stanchions
headed by a moulded rim; iron shoe. The original bright
green paint survives beneath the later coat of black
l. 92

Lent by Mr and Mrs Robin Compton (Newby Hall)

20

20 Fender
c. 1800
Bright steel and brass with an iron shoe
A very good example of well moulded steelwork
combined with studding and the use of smart ornamental
brass ware — the feet and applied anthemion ornament
framed in squares
l. 135

Lent by Mr and Mrs Robin Compton (Newby Hall)

21 Standard fender
Early 19th century
Brass and polished steel
The machine-cut openwork grille still bears traces of the
original green paint; brass mouldings and ball feet (one

21

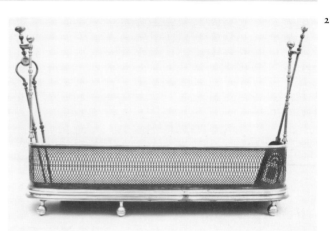

22

22 Standard fender
In the style of George Bullock, 1823–24
Brass, pewter and steel
The running pattern is executed in brass and pewter in
the manner of buhlwork, a decorative treatment repeated
on the front consoles of the fire grate; steel standards.
Identical to the fender and grate in the adjoining library.
Associated with Lewis Wyatt's alterations to Heaton
Hall in 1823–24
l. 105

Lent by Manchester City Art Galleries (Heaton Hall)

23 Hanging fire guard
19th century, first half
Brass and wrought iron
The curved frame supports a brass wire lattice and is
fitted with adjustable fire bar hooks
h. 52

Lent by Mr and Mrs Robin Compton (Newby Hall)

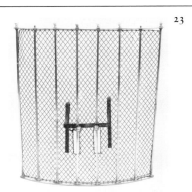

23

FIRE IRONS

Wood-burning fires required a pair of widely splayed log
tongs with claw terminals and a long-handled log fork,
but for coal a shovel, tongs and poker were standard
items of equipment. At Ham House in the 1670s, where
most of the hearths were provided with a fire pan for
burning charcoal, a shovel and tongs sufficed (Cat. 24)
but at Dyrham (1710) and Kiveton (1727) a full set of
implements accompanied most grates. They were often
decoratively styled, the ornamental elaboration of finials
providing the best clue as to date. At Harewood (1795)
the fire irons in six of the State apartments included a
'Hearth Rook', this tool was almost certainly an iron key
used for adjusting a Register grate of which a solitary
example has been identified (Cat. 29).

At Ham many fire irons, like the rest of the chimney
furniture sported silver mounts. The Marquess of
Exeter's collection at Burghley contains a magnificent set
of solid silver implements — the tongs and shovel hall-
marked for 1674, the poker added by Paul Storr in 1815.
These were obviously intended for display rather than
use. Wrought iron was gradually replaced in the early
18th century by brass and later polished steel. Many
neoclassical sets such as those from Osterley (Cats 31 and
33) were carefully designed to match decorative finials on
fire grates and might be enriched with bright-cut
engraving. A fine set with 'flaming tops' made by Henry
Tobin of Leeds for Harewood in 1772 has been identified
(Cat. 30). The blades of early shovels were boldly flared,
they later became shallower and straighter and in the
Adam period were often pierced with neat open-work
patterns — this treatment was known at the time as
'grating'.

At Ham House the fire irons were suspended by
terminal rings from elegant silver hooks flanking the
fireplace, later jamb crooks (see illustration on title page)
were fixed to the sides of chimney pieces so that the tools
could be propped upright. There is also pictorial evidence
that the irons were sometimes paraded in a row leaning
against the front bars of empty grates. About 1800 short
standards headed by C-scrolls were frequently slotted
into the returns of fenders to support the implements
(Cat. 21). All sources point to fire irons standing erect in a
corner of the hearth until about 1830 when an alternative
fashion emerged for laying fire tools almost horizontally
on the hearthstone the ends lodged on low rests.

The fashion for baronial interiors which started in the
Regency period brought with it a demand for log tongs
and fire forks (Cats 35 and 36).

24 Tongs and shovel
c. 1675
Iron and silver
The shafts with bobbin-style sections are ornamented
with leafy bulbous mounts; the tongs display finely

24

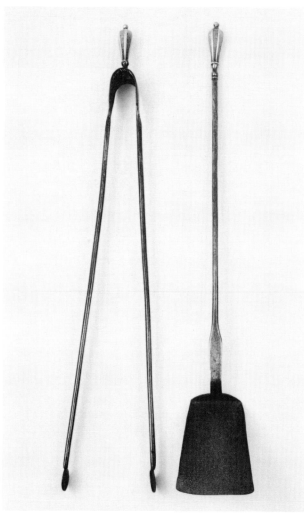

25

wrought scrolls and the blade of the shovel is deeply dished and splayed with cut-work corners
l. 82

Sets of shovel and tongs 'done wt silver' are listed in several rooms in the Ham inventories of 1677, 1679 and 1683

Lent by the Trustees of the Victoria & Albert Museum (Ham House)

25 Tongs and shovel
Late 17th century
Steel and brass
The tongs are sprung, not hinged and the flanged shovel blade is set at an angle to the handle, probably for scooping up charcoal. The hexagonal brass knobs with hatched facets are shaped like oriental vases which were fashionable collectors' items at the time
l. 84 (shovel)

Lent by the National Trust (Knole)

26 Set of fire irons
17th century, second half
Steel
The shafts are swelled towards the tops and have mushroom finials, the flared shovel blade has deeply

26

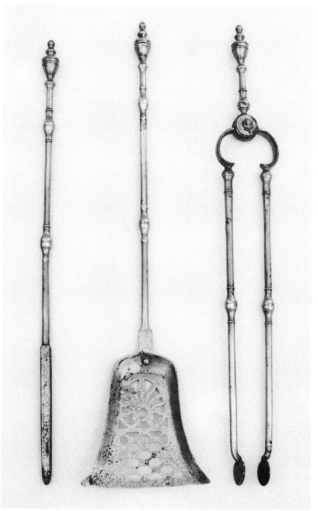

27

splayed sides. The unusually small size and pin hinge on the tongs are indications of an early date
l. 54 (shovel)

Lent by the National Trust (Knole)

27 Set of fire irons
Attributed to Tobin of Leeds, *c.* 1770
Steel with vase finials
The shovel has been cut down by about 3.5 cm at the bottom. Of almost identical pattern (except for the finials) to Cat. 28 from Newby Hall where Tobin also worked
l. 76 (shovel)

Lent by the Earl of Harewood (Harewood House)

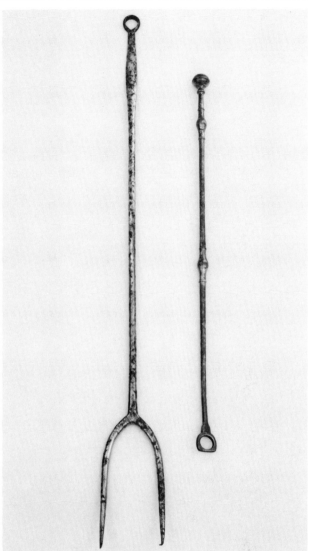

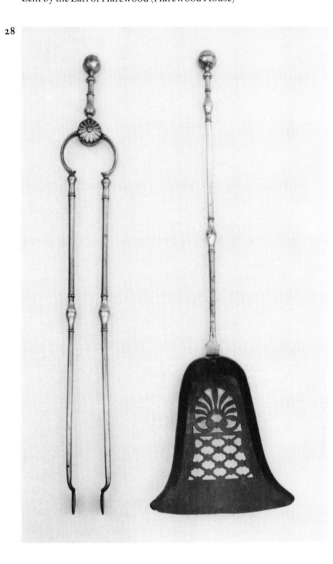

28 Shovel and tongs
Attributed to Tobin of Leeds, *c.* 1770
Steel, with facetted acorn finials
Of virtually identical pattern (excepting the finials) to Cat. 27 from Harewood House; it is likely that both sets are by Tobin who worked at Harewood and Newby
l. 75 (tongs)

Lent by Mr and Mrs Robin Compton (Newby Hall)

29 Hearth rook
Attributed to Tobin of Leeds, *c.* 1770
Polished steel
'Hearth rooks' are recorded amongst items of chimney furniture in many of the State Rooms at Harewood House in the 1795 inventory. They were 'keys' used for adjusting register grates. Since many of the grates were installed by Tobin of Leeds around 1770 it is likely that he also supplied these implements of which this is a solitary survivor. The shaft is closely similar to other irons associated with Tobin's commission
l. 71

Lent by Earl of Harewood (Harewood House)

30

31

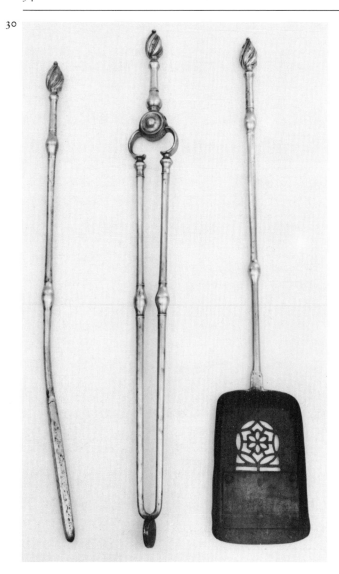

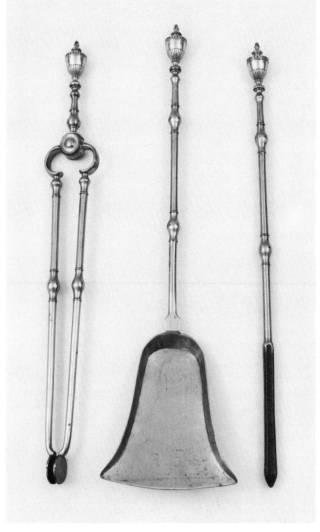

30 Set of fire irons
Attributed to Tobin of Leeds, *c.* 1772
Bright steel with wrythen flame finials
The 'grated' shovel is decorated with an openwork rose
(lower part repaired)
Henry Tobin invoiced several 'case hardened' fire irons
'with flaming tops' and 'grated' shovels to Edwin
Lascelles of Harewood House in 1772. This is almost
certainly one of the documented sets
l. 85 (tongs)

Lent by the Earl of Harewood (Harewood House)

31 Set of fire irons
c. 1773
Polished steel and paktong
From the drawing room at Osterley (see Cat. 8). The
shafts have two bulbous sections and terminate in finely
cast golden paktong vases which correspond to the finials
on the grate. The vases are detailed with pearl beading,
gadrooning, Vitruvian scrolls and have pineapple finials.
The poker has an iron tip and the blade and lower stem of
the shovel have been replaced
h. 80 (shovel)

Lent by the Trustees of the Victoria & Albert Museum (Osterley Park)

32

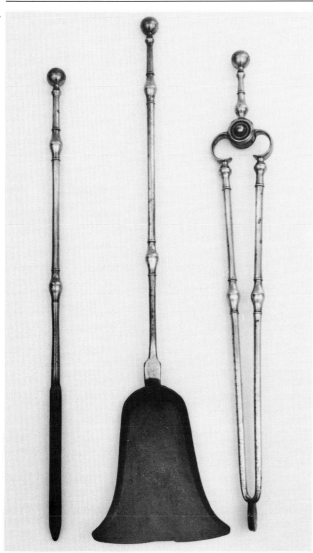

33

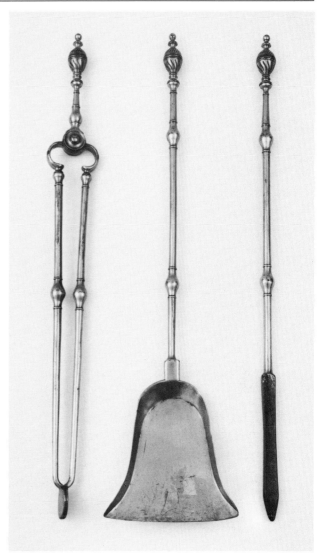

32 Set of fire irons
Attributed to Tobin or Rodgers of Leeds, *c.* 1770–75
Steel with ball finials
Both these Leeds whitesmiths were supplying hearth
furniture to Newby Hall in the 1770s
l. 86 (shovel)

Lent by Mr and Mrs Robin Compton (Newby Hall)

33 Set of fire irons (one of a pair)
c. 1775
Polished steel
From the library at Osterley (see Cat. 10). The shafts have
two bulbous sections and terminate in vases decorated
with wrythen flutes, a guilloche band and ball finials
which match the ornamental vases on the grate. The
poker has an iron tip
h. 85 (shovel)

Lent by the Trustees of the Victoria & Albert Museum (Osterley Park)

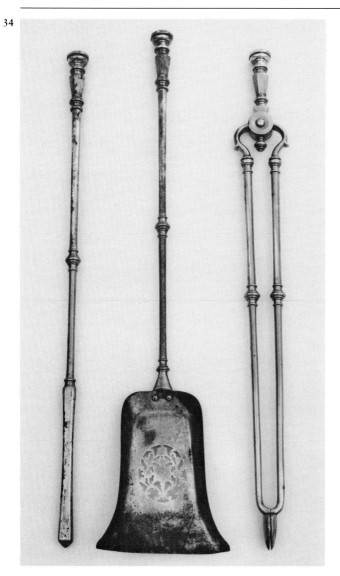

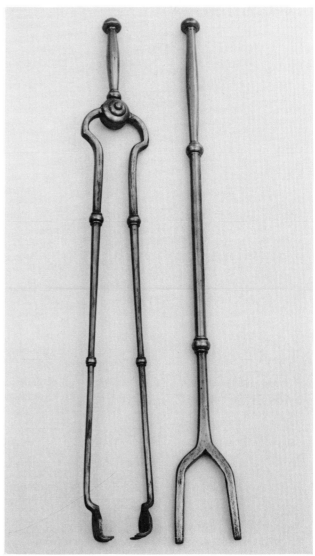

34 Set of fire irons
Probably late 18th century
Polished steel with octagonal brass finials
The brass terminals and lack of wear on the blade of the
shovel raise the possibility that these implements are of
late Victorian date when many of the hearths at
Harewood were re-equipped
l. 89 (shovel)

Lent by the Earl of Harewood (Harewood House)

35 Log fork
Probably early 19th century
Polished steel
Log forks (and tongs) seem to have reappeared with the
Regency fashion for baronial interior decoration
l. 90

Lent by Mr and Mrs Robin Compton (Newby Hall)

36 Fire fork and log tongs
c. 1825
Bright steel
One of two sets which correspond to a design attributed
to Richard Bridgens inscribed: 'Entrance Hall|1824'.
Commissioned by James Watt for Aston Hall,
Birmingham
Furniture History, XV (1979), pls 107A and B
l. 106

Lent by Birmingham Museums and Art Gallery (Aston Hall)

HEARTH BRUSHES AND BROOMS

These implements regularly occur in inventories, but surviving examples of any age are virtually non-existent. The only venerable specimen is the well known one at Ham House of *c.* 1675 overlaid with embossed silver (Cat. 37). Inventory descriptions are always very bare so it is fortunate that two mid-18th century engravings of a 'brush' and a 'broom' have been traced. Edwards and Darly's *New Book of Chinese Designs*, 1754, pl. 64 shows a hearth brush with a japanned back (Fig. 56) while W. & J. Welldon's *The Smith's Right Hand*, 1765, pl. 9 portrays a broom with a circular head similar to the Ham example (Fig. 23). They were clearly inexpensive, items for in 1757 Maurice Tobin charged Edwin Lascelles as follows:

1 Gilt Hearth Brush	1/4d
1 Wallnut Do	1/3d
1 Painted Do	10d

In 1797 Gillows supplied Lord Gage of Firle Place with '2 hearth Brooms finish'd black & Gold 10/–', a finish which matched the firescreens. Evidence of the increased attention paid to hearth utensils during the Regency period is a design for Gothic fire irons, a broom and pair of bellows which A. C. Pugin contributed to Ackermann's *Repository of Arts* for September 1827.

37 Hearth broom
c. 1675
Silver (maker's mark s s over a star)
The circular domed head ornamented with embossed acanthus fronds houses a wooden stock set with bristles; tubular, tapered handle ending in a cable-twist suspension ring; some rooms at Ham House still preserve silver hooks by the chimneypiece from which fire implements were hung
l. 61
Silver hearth brooms are recorded in several of the best interiors in the Ham inventories of 1677, 1679 and 1683
Lent by the Trustees of the Victoria & Albert Museum (Ham House)

BELLOWS

Traditional pear-shaped bellows have a long history stretching well back into the Middle Ages, but the earliest extant examples date from about 1600. After the Restoration they were often lavishly decorated, throughout the 18th century they seem to have been regarded as ultility articles and are generally plainly styled but during the Regency period a taste for fanciful treatment re-emerged.

At Ham House, where everything was ostentatiously splendid, several suites of silver mounted chimney furniture were ordered about 1675. One pair of bellows from this commission survives, faced on each side with elaborately pierced, embossed and chased silver bearing the cypher and coronet of the Duchess of Lauderdale (Cat. 39). The only other equally luxurious silver bellows are at the Ashmolean Museum, Oxford. Other forms of decoration employed at this time included colourful marquetry (Cat. 40), elaborate carving (Cat. 38) and stumpwork. The so-called 'Queen Anne' reaction against sumptuous ornament ushered in an age when bellows were severely plain, the board with the vent hole being faced with figured veneers, the other side often bearing shallow ring turning (Cat. 41), japanned examples were also popular. Elm was the preferred timber for rustic bellows. None are mentioned in Chippendale's surviving bills which suggests that they were usually made by specialist tradesmen. However, Gillows' invoice of 1797 to Lord Gage of Firle Park includes 'a pr of Sattinwood French Bellows 12s 6d | a pr of Mahogany Do 9s 6d'.

The Regency period witnessed a revival of the fashion for pretty bellows; some were attractively japanned in black and gold with chinoiseries subjects (Cat. 42) others received pen-work decoration (V & A E1687–1963) while Peterborough museum contains examples decorated by French prisoners of war with straw marquetry (*Connoisseur*, XXVII, (1910), p. 50). Improved tech-

nology introduced wheel action bellows operating a fan (Cat. 44) and standing bellows pumped by a handle (Cat. 43).

38 Bellows

Late 17th century
Walnut and oak with a brass nozzle
The walnut front board is richly carved with the arms of Copelston, County Devon amid scrolled acanthus fronds with a winged cherub's head at the bottom. They are — Argent a chevron engrailed gules between three leopard's faces. Crest: a demi-tiger gules, tufted and maned or. The oak back board is pierced by a circular vent hole
l. 60

Lent by Mr and Mrs E. Hall

38

39

39 Bellows
c. 1675
Various woods and silver
Maker's mark s s over a star
Oak boards, the front faced with an elaborately pierced
and chased foliate pattern silver mount centering on a
cartouche engraved with the monogram E L beneath a
Ducal coronet; the back board, finely decorated with
floral marquetry executed in coloured woods and green

40

41

stained ivory on an ebony ground centres on a vent hole
covered by a perforated silver acanthus boss; the handles,
also sheathed in silver, have an eye for a suspension ring;
silver nozzle. Illustrated in colour on the back cover
l. 52

Made for Elizabeth, Duchess of Lauderdale. Silver
bellows are recorded in a few of the principal apartments
at Ham in the inventories of 1677, 1679 and 1683

Lent by the Trustees of the Victoria & Albert Museum (Ham House)

40 Bellows
Late 17th century
Walnut decorated with various stained and shaded
woods including ivory elements, the nozzle, handles and
pierced monogram mounted over the vent hole are of
silver
Marquetry bellows are very rare, the silver fitments
emphasize the luxurious quality of this pair. Both sides

are faced with floral designs. Since ornamental vases of flowers were often stationed in empty hearths this theme was particularly appropriate
l. 56

Lent by Mr and Mrs Robin Compton (Newby Hall)

41 Bellows
18th century, first half
Walnut with leather gussets and a brass nozzle; the solid front board is ornamented with traditional concentric turning, the back, veneered with figured walnut centres on a vent hole
l. 57

Leeds City Art Galleries (Temple Newsam)

42

42 Bellows
Early 19th century
Japanned boards, the front decorated with a chinoiserie scene in gold on a black ground; brass nozzle
l. 30

Lent by Robert Aagaard

43

43 Standing bellows
Early 19th century
Mahogany
Of rectangular 'box' design; the frame supports a fixed lower and movable upper board joined by the leather gusset, the top is inlaid with two shamrock leaves. By pumping a turned ebony handle draught is expelled through the metal nozzle (a re-used spigot)
h. 31, l. 29

Lent by the National Trust (Knole)

44

44 Wheel bellows
Early 19th century
The tin boxing with brass trims houses a fan operated by a cord drive passing over a brass wheel; the mahogany board is inlaid with ivory and has a circular brass spy-hole on the underside
l. 70

This hand-held specimen is designed to hang up, others were mounted on low stands. There is a good brass example at Newby Hall, Yorkshire

Lent by York Castle Museum

COAL BOXES AND COAL SCUTTLES

References in the Ham House inventories of 1677 and 1679 suggest that in some rooms coal may have been kept in a fireside basket. Such receptacles can hardly have been satisfactory and special containers for holding coal made an appearance soon afterwards. In 1715 Lady Grissel Baille of Jerviswood purchased 'ane yron coll basket £3. 3s' and 'a coper scuttel' (*Dictionary of English Furniture*). In view of the high price it is likely the coal basket was a type of grate and this may be true also of the Ham references, however, the second item was certainly

a type of coal bucket. The consistent absence of coal scuttles or boxes from hearth furniture listed in 18th century inventories shows they were not then recognized accessories. This is confirmed by Swift's *Directions to Servants* of 1729 which mentions coal boxes as 'unsightly Things' liable to be left about by housemaids after making up the fire.

The trade card of Alexander Wetherstone, carpenter, joiner and turner of London, *c.* 1760 advertises 'Tin Coal Scoops' and 'Tind Scuttles' while the Newby Hall inventory of 1792 records '3 copper coal skuttles' in a store room. At Harewood in 1795 the candlestick cleaning room contained '15 Iron Coal Pans, 5 Copper Do'. During the Regency period smart coal boxes became an acceptable article of chimney furniture. They were usually of tinned steel japanned black with gilt decoration and cast ornaments. The sarcophagus-shaped example probably designed by Richard Bridgens for Aston Hall (Cat. 45) is typical of these new arrivals, others survive at Harewood House (Cats 46 and 47) and Burghley House. Between 1811–14 Feltham supplied 'Two Japan Coal Scuttles | 3 Copper Coal Hods' to Carlton House, while in 1819 Thomason & Jones of Birmingham provided '12 Copper Coal Scuttles' to the same establishment (p. 71).

45

45 Coal box with hinged lid
Richard Harbourn, Birmingham, *c.* 1825
Sheet iron with cast details, painted black
The only survivor of several sarcophagus-shaped coal boxes ordered by James Watt for Aston Hall about 1824.

46

47

It corresponds to a design attributed to Richard Bridgens inscribed: 'Coal Box | For the Gt Library | Aston Hall | Harbourn Bull St'. Richard Harbourn is recorded in Wrightson's *Birmingham Directory*, 1821, as trading in Bull Street as ironmonger, locksmith, bell hanger and stove grate maker
h. 68, l. 79

Lent by Birmingham Museums and Art Gallery (Aston Hall)

46 Coal box

Japanned steel, *c.* 1830
Sarcophagus shaped with a high domed cover japanned black with gilt bands, cast iron mask lifting handles and paw feet
h. 50, l. 45

Lent by the Earl of Harewood (Harewood House)

47 Coal box

Japanned steel, *c.* 1840–50
Oval with a domed cover japanned black with gilt details; zinc liner. The cast handle and feet display a hybrid Regency/rococo-revival character suggesting the period of Sir Charles Barry's improvements at Harewood House during the 1840s
h. 50, l. 54

Lent by the Earl of Harewood (Harewood House)

CATS

These intriguing domestic items were made either of metal or from timber suitable for turning such as mahogany, cherry or ebonized wood. They stood near the fire and served as stands to keep plates of muffins or toast warm. One is shown in Gillray's print titled *Toasting Muffins*, 1791. The plate was supported on the tips of the arms as portrayed in Rowlandson's humorous drawing *The Catastrophe*, *c.* 1800 (Fig. 13). Another is depicted in his sketch *The Challenge*: both are in the collection of Boston Public Library. William Tonks & Sons of Birmingham illustrated a brass 'Cat or Plate

Fig. 13 T. Rowlandson, 'The Catastrophe', c.1800 showing a cat supporting a plate of muffins
Boston Public Library, the Wiggin Collection

stand' of classic form in their metalwork pattern book of 1886 priced 3s 10d each (Castle Museum, York) — a salutary warning that some cats are not all that old.

The name is thought to have been inspired either by its customary fireside place or from its design of six tripod spokes springing from a central ball so that it always as it were fell on its feet. J. Wright's *Dialect Dictionary* quotes a Shropshire source which indicates that cats were found in quite humble homes 'I'll butter the flaps straight off the backs twun, if you fetch me a plate an' a cat to put it on they'n keep whot till tay'.

Wooden examples are comparatively common, the orb (or occasionally vase-shaped hubs) frequently being made in two halves to revolve on a central pin and the arms styled with simulated bamboo, spiral twist or ridge turnings. Some examples are set on cabriole or splayed tripod bases and are thus non-reversible The OED records the earliest usage as 1806 but Ralph Edward's in the *Dictionary of English Furniture* notes that the Joiner's Company purchased two mahogany cats in 1798–99. Documentary references are scarce — they were probably listed as trivets in many inventories — but

most seem to possess a Regency character. Edward Pinto in *Treen and Other Wooden Bygones* insists that the glued joints (some arms are screwed into the body) could not have withstood the heat of a fire and suggests they functioned as stands for workbaskets or flower bowls. They may sometimes have served such secondary purposes but his case remains unproven.

49

49 Cat
Early 19th century
Iron, painted black
The central stem, decorated in the manner of bobbin turning, has an orb at each end from which spring three spiral twist arms terminating in balls
h. 32

Lent by the Trustees of the Victoria & Albert Museum

48

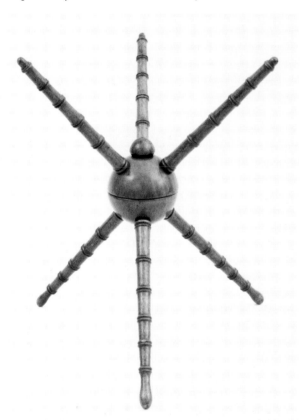

48 Cat
Early 19th century
Walnut, in the form of a double tripod stand with six spokes that radiate like a star from a central sphere, the two halves of which are united by a screw peg that allows them to revolve
h. 40

Leeds City Art Galleries (Temple Newsam)

TRIVETS

50 Trivet
Engraved brass, c. 1770
Of tripod form with prongs to hook over the top fire bar. Many trivets have survived but it would be hard to find a more elegantly styled example
h. 33

Lent by Mr and Mrs Robin Compton (Newby Hall)

51 Hanging trivet
19th century, first half
Brass, in the form of a ring with three dished spokes centering on a rose and a hinged brace terminating in

50

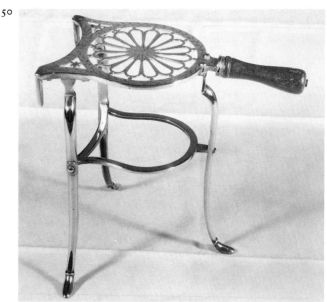

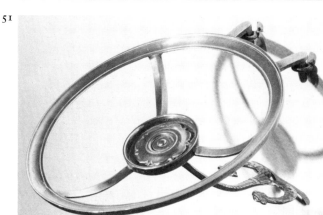

51

52

53

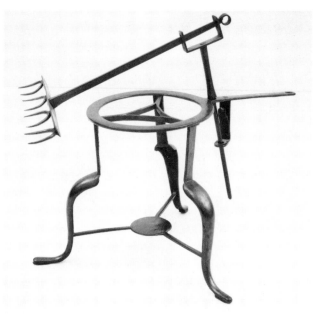

paired eagle-head scrolls; the two lugs are for hooking over the top of a fender
diam. 18

Leeds City Art Galleries (Temple Newsam)

52 Fire bar trivet
Cast-iron, *c.* 1840
Lettered: 'A KENRICK & SONS No 8'
In the form of an openwork anthemion with fire-bar hooks and an adjustable arm
diam. 17

Lent by the Earl of Harewood (Harewood House)

53 Trivet toaster
Probably 19th century, first half
Iron, with adjustable fork set with four double prongs, mounted on a circular trivet raised on three cabriole legs united by cross stretchers
h. 40

Lent by York Castle Museum

CHAIR BACK SCREENS

Although conventional fire screens designed to shield the face have been purposely omitted from this survey, another class of screen made to protect the back from heat is featured because survivors are exceedingly rare and this seemed a good chance to publish a note on the subject.

When open coal fires were lit in dining rooms it was found that those who sat with their backs to the fire

needed a screen 'to prevent the unpleasant effects of this situation'. Thus, the chair back screen was an item of dining room furniture. One of the earliest references to these accessories occurs in a Gillows bill of 1779 invoicing 'six neat fire screens to drop upon the backs of Chairs . . . upon frames covered with strong paper'. ordered for the dining room at Heaton Hall. The Harewood House inventory of 1795 records in a closet adjoining the dining room '4 chair back fire screens', examples are also listed at Audley End in 1797 while in

1810 Gillows despatched '4 chair back screens covered in crimson Tammy' and 16 dining chairs to Parlington Hall, Yorkshire.

J. C. Loudon's *Encyclopedia of Cottage, Farm and Villa Architecture and Furniture*, 1833 illustrates a large circular screen of woven straw 'with a hook by which it is hung on the back of a chair' (Fig. 14). Thomas Walker and Mrs Parker, co-authors of *An Encyclopedia of Domestic Economy*, c. 1840, portrayed a rectangular screen with rounded corners, stating 'The simplest and one that frequently answers the purpose, is a flat mat worked of willow that is hung on the back of each chair requiring such defence'. Other pictorial evidence includes a single plate in W. Smee & Son's trade catalogue, c. 1860 showing three 'fancy' basket work examples.

It is likely that the use of chair back screens first became fashionable during the 1770s, reached a peak of popularity about 1800, remained in demand throughout the Regency period and finally fell into disuse around the time of the Great War. One of their last appearances must surely be in the *Art Wicker Furniture Catalogue* issued by Morris, Wilkinson & Co., Nottingham in 1909 where white 'cushion' shaped screens are advertized at 12s, 15s and 20s per pair. Wicker wash stand splash-backs are now similarly obsolete and scarce so it may be worth mentioning the existence of fine specimens at Raby Castle, Co. Durham and Harewood House.

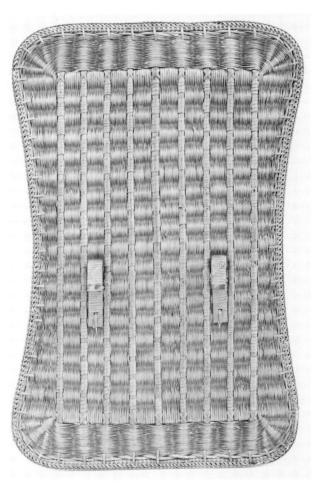

54

54 Chair back screen
Late 19th century
Basketwork with two metal hooks
Size 70 × 48

Leeds City Art Galleries (Temple Newsam)

Fig. 14 Chair back screen of woven straw, from J. C. Loudon's 'Encyclopedia', 1833

CHIMNEY BOARDS

Chimney or fireboards, sometimes known as 'chimney stops', were employed to close gloomy looking fireplace openings during the summer or when a room was not in regular use. They were both practical and decorative for, by sealing off the space soot and draughts were excluded, while most were attractively styled, often to harmonise with the decor. Information about them is widely scattered, so an effort has been made to round up published material while adding a few new facts.

Late 17th century continental chimney boards survive, thus it is likely that they were also known in fashionable English homes, but the earliest record so far traced for their use in this country is a reference in the Kiveton inventory of 1727 to eleven stored in a coal closet. There is also an interesting bill dated 1730 from the cabinet maker George Nix to the Earl of Dysart at Ham House for supplying 'a white board for a Chimney grownded for Japaning 12/–'. This suggests it was intended to decorate in the Chinese taste possibly by the ladies of the house: oriental themes were certainly favoured later in the century. When Dr Pococke visited Longford Castle in 1754 he noted 'the chimney boards through the house are made of Chinese pictures, which show several of their customs'. Although no chinoiserie specimens seem to survive they are depicted in various portraits by Arthur Devis and a trade card issued about 1760 by Matthias Darly, painter, engraver and paper stainer, is decorated with two ornamented in the Chinese taste; the text announced that he stocked 'Chimney Boards &c Neatly fitted up with Painting or Stainings in the Modern, Gothic or Chinese Taste'. Hand-painted oriental wallpaper was of course very popular for facing or backing firescreens at this date.

Thomas Chippendale was sometimes commissioned to supply routine chimney boards in his capacity as general house furnisher. For instance, in 1760 Sir William Robinson was provided with '2 Chimney Boards fitted to your Chimneys cover'd wt Crimson flock paper upon canvas to match the room wt Turnbuckles etc £1 2s od' and in 1767 Sir Rowland Winn of Nostell Priory paid him for 'covering 9 Chimney bords with blue verditer paper & putting boarders round ditto £1 16s od': a year later he recovered and fitted a further 8 with new turnbuckles (knobs with swivel arms to keep the boards in place). Zoffany's well-known portrait of Sir Lawrence Dundas with his grandson in the library at 19 Arlington Street shows a chimneypiece closed by a board covered with plain paper.

A study of furniture bills suggests either that fashionable cabinetmakers seldom received orders to supply these articles or that they were not regarded as essential items of equipment in well appointed rooms. Inventories confirm that many owners thought of them as optional extras, for there is no evience for their use at Harewood house (1795), Newby (1792), Appuldurcombe (1780) or Temple Newsam (1808) while the

Osterley inventory of 1782 records ten (all in bed or dressing rooms), five were commissioned for the State apartments at Audley End in 1769 and they are also found at Burghley in 1804. Some patrons, no doubt encouraged by their architect, spent considerable sums on impressive boards. At Osterley Robert Adam was paid for designing two very sophisticated examples (Cats 63 and 64) and in 1769 Biagio Rebecca painted five at a cost of twenty guineas for Audley End, four of which survive (Cats 57–60).

On occasion the embellishment of chimney boards was taken up by ladies as a fashionable pastime. In 1783 Miss Hamilton decorated one for her hostess the Duchess of Portland: 'Mr Levers, ye house steward, came to me and bought me ye chimney-board he had made for ye Library, wch I had promised ye Dss to cover with prints'. She also repaired a board ordered by Mrs Delany with 'color'd paper, vases antique figures, &c' (probably purchased from a print seller). An example at Heveningham is faced with prints, although this was doubtless the work of a professional decorator. At Lacock Abbey a fireplace in the South Gallery is closed by a cast-iron plate datable to about 1830.

There were two ways of making boards, they could be either of solid framed panel or plank construction or the canvas was mounted on a stretcher like an easel painting. The timber foundation might be either japanned, covered with wallpaper (Cats 61 and 62), tapestry, gilt leather, or fine art prints: some were painted, either directly onto the woods (Cats 55 and 56) or on canvas (Cats 57–60 and 63–65). Painted subjects ranged from *trompe l'œil* fire

55

grates with or without a fire burning (Cat. 65), representations of vases of flowers which were often in reality placed on the hearth (Cat. 55 and 56) or ambitious neoclassical compositions devised to complement the wall treatment (Cat. 64) or relate to a chimney garniture or decorative elements such as vases stationed in the room (Cat. 57). Fine examples portraying vases of flowers survive at Dunster Castle, Somerset and at Victor Hugo's house on Guernsey. This type has sometimes at a later date been framed and hung as a still life painting, there is one such at Burghley.

A review of the evidence indicates that the use of chimney boards was never widespread in England, they seem to have been restricted to a minority of country houses, although a few unprovenanced 'manor house' examples are known. They were certainly far more popular in America, becoming a branch of folk art.

56

55 Chimney board

c. 1700
Pine, of plank construction with cross battens, the front, painted in oils, portrays a blue and white delftware vase containing tulips, carnations and other garden flowers on a black ground; the border represents a tiled fireplace surround decorated with pots of flowers executed in blue on a white ground. The subject was inspired by the custom of placing vases of flowers on the hearth during summertime
Size: 98 × 78

Lent by the Trustees of the Victoria & Albert Museum

56 Chimney board

Painted pine, *c.* 1760
Of plank construction with two cross battens; the top rail is fitted with a turn-buckle. Painted with a rococo vase containing flowers standing in a niche with a shell in the arch. The board has been extended more than once at the edges
Original size: 90 × 71

Lent by Roger Warner, Burford

57 Chimney board

Biagio Rebecca, 1769
Canvas, mounted on a pine frame and painted in oils with a marble antique vase on a green ground framed by a white waterleaf border
Size: 125 × 152

Documentation: 'Audley End Decr 12. 1769 | Reciev'd of Sir John G Griffin | Twenty Guineas for painting Five Chimney | Boards, & mending four full length | Pictures —Biagio Rebecca.'
This board was commissioned for the dining parlour and is recorded in the 1797 inventory as 'a painted Chimney stop by Rebecca'. Adam's original watercolour designs for the room shows that it was painted pea green and the 1797 schedule records that it contained 'Four florentine Vases on pedestals'; the leaf border echoes the moulding of the chimney cornice. Thus, the chimney board was

57

carefully styled to harmonise with the decor. Sally MacDonald has pointed out that the source for this design is the Athenian vase in the Villa Borghese, one of the most admired of antique marble vases. Rebecca could have seen engravings of it or the alabaster copy at Houghton Hall or a version at Coade's Manufactory

Lent by R. H. L. Neville

58 Chimney board

Biagio Rebecca, 1769
Canvas, mounted on a pine stretcher and painted in oils with a marble altar and beribboned oak swags on a grey ground with a bead and billet border
Size: 125 × 149

Documentation: see Cat. 57
This board was almost certainly commissioned for the Library since the ground colour approximates to that of the six Cipriani frieze panels designed for this interior

Lent by R. H. L. Neville

58

60

59

surrounded by a classical border executed in grisaille on a blue ground

Size: 118 × 123

Documentation: see Cat. 57
Probably ordered for the North Parlour (Supper Room) which was decorated with a pale blue colour scheme and in 1797 contained 'a Chimney stop (Rebecca)'

Lent by R. H. L. Neville

61

59 Chimney board

Biagio Rebecca, 1769
Canvas, mounted on a pine stretcher and painted in oils with a roundel representing two cupids with foliate spandrels; depicted in white on a blue ground. Later gilt frame

Size: 110 × 110

Documentation: see Cat. 57
Probably commissioned for Lord Howard's Writing Room which in the 1797 inventory contained 'A Painted Chimney Stop — Rebecca'. and had pale blue paintwork and curtains

Lent by R. H. L. Neville

60 Chimney board

Biagio Rebecca, 1769
Canvas, mounted on a pine stretcher and painted in oils with a representation of an antique marble relief

61 Chimney board

c. 1775
The carcase, constructed of pine planks, is lined with canvas and faced with painted paper. The floral chinoiserie design in green, blue and pink on a buff ground is closely related to the Oriental painted bed hangings in the Taffeta Bedchamber at Osterley; however, it fits the fireplace in the 'India Paper Dressing

Room' which contained a 'Chimney board' when the 1782 inventory was compiled
Size: 108 × 102

Lent by the Trustees of the Victoria & Albert Museum (Osterley Park)

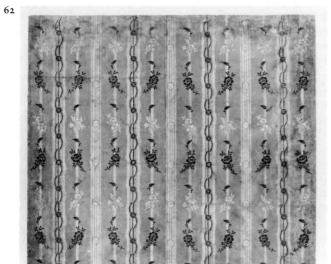

62 Chimney board

c. 1775
The solid pine board of framed panel construction is covered with blue wallpaper printed with a black and white striped pattern. The 1782 Osterley inventory records 'A Chimney Board covered with Paper' in several upstairs rooms, but the precise location of this example has not been established. It is likely that the board matched the wallpaper hung in the room
Size: 103 × 102

Lent by the Trustees of the Victoria & Albert Museum (Osterley Park)

63 Chimney board

Designed by Robert Adam, 1778
Pine carcase of framed flush panel construction covered with canvas painted in oils with a decorative scheme which is related to neoclassical elements elsewhere in the room, especially the ceiling ornament. The pictorial lunette represents 'Sleep'. The pale greyish ground and bottom border may provide a clue to the original colour scheme of the skirting and dado. Oval cast brass knob in the form of a patera. Recorded in the 1782 Osterley inventory (State Bedroom): 'A chimney board covered with Paper painted with Etruscan ornaments' (no grate is listed)
Size: 117 × 126

The coloured design for this board is in the Soane Museum, Adam drawings, XVII, no. 138, dated 22 August 1778; there is another sketch in pencil.

Lent by the Trustees of the Victoria & Albert Museum (Osterley Park)

64 Chimney board

Designed by Robert Adam, 1777
Pine carcase of framed flush panel construction covered with canvas painted in oils with a neoclassical composition in colours on a blue-grey ground with a paler strip at the bottom; cast brass knob in the form of an oval patera. The ornament relates very closely to the prevailing decor. Recorded in the 1782 Osterley inventory (Etruscan Dressing Room): 'The Room hung with Canvas and Paper and very elegantly painted with Etruscan ornaments and Chimney board ditto.'
Size: 117 × 127

Adam's design is in the Soane Museum, XVII, no. 137, dated 2 June 1777; there is also a pencil sketch (XXIV, no. 221) featuring an alternative proposal on the right hand side

Lent by the Trustees of the Victoria & Albert Museum (Osterley Park)

65 Chimney board

c. 1780

Canvas, painted in oils with a representation of a neo-classical grate in a fireplace with marble slips. Mounted on a new stretcher, the lower part restored

Size: 116 × 118

Leeds City Art Galleries (Temple Newsam)

PRINTED AND MANUSCRIPT DESIGNS

These visual sources comprise three classes of material. Firstly, pattern books, trade catalogues and drawings produced by working smiths and ironmongers. Secondly, volumes of engravings and collections of designs by furniture makers which include representations of chimney furniture. Thirdly, grates, etc. designed by professional architects or decorators. These groups will be considered in turn.

DESIGNS BY SMITHS AND IRONMONGERS

In 1765 William and John Welldon published a volume titled *The Smith's Right Hand or a Complete Guide to the Various Branches of all Sorts of Iron Work*, part 1 of which, devoted entirely to grates, is of such outstanding interest that all 16 plates, plus one from a later section illustrating fenders, are reproduced here from a copy in the Victoria & Albert Museum Library (Figs 15–31). The title page of the first part announced that it contained:

Near FORTY genteel, new and beautiful DESIGNS, for

PHILADELPHIA,	MODERN,
VENITIAN,	ORNAMENTAL,
CHINESE,	BATH and
GOTHIC,	FRENCH STOVES

Calculated for the Universal USE of

STOVE GRATE MAKERS,	BRAZIERS
SMITHS,	FORGERS,
IRONMONGERS,	JAPANNERS, &c.

And particularly intended to furnish NOBLEMEN and GENTLEMEN with Variety of CHOICE

Amongst the DESIGNS published in this Book is a beautiful BATH Stove, executed at a Gentleman's House near BOND–STREET; and which is universally allowed to be the only method to prevent Chimneys from smoking at all Times, and during all weather.

The Whole neatly ENGRAVED from the Original DRAWINGS, made

By Messrs. W. and J. WELLDON, Smiths

LONDON

Printed for HENRY WEBLEY, in Holborn, near Chancery-Lane

MDCCLXV

Plates 1 and 2 combine alternative treatments for Venetian Stoves in the same design. The two pictorial cartouches on the second plate are copied directly from Thomas Johnson's suite of engravings on six leaves titled *A New Book of Ornaments . . . Designed for Tablets & Friezes for Chimney-Pieces*, 1762. The Philadelphia Stoves on pl. 6 appear to be indistinguishable from the previous Venetian Stoves and the Bath Stoves on pl. 7 show little advance on the example in Ince & Mayhew's *Universal System* (perhaps they solicited this design from the Welldons). The authors were very proud of the specimen on pl. 8 claiming that it solved the perennial problem of smoking chimneys, but their pl. 9 featuring 'Stove Grates with Gothick Frets' is of keener interest because it also depicts a full range of implements. The remaining designs on pls 10–16 form an excellent anthology of elaborate stove grates with fancy names, while pl. 21 in the following part illustrates eight fenders. Altogether this is a capital collection.

Fig. 15 W & J Welldon, 1765, pl. 1, Venetian Stoves

Fig. 16 W & J Welldon, 1765, pl. 2, Venetian Stoves

Fig. 17   W & J Welldon, 1765, pl.3, Venetian Stoves

Fig. 18   W & J Welldon, 1765, pl.4, Venetian Stoves

Fig. 19   W & J Welldon, 1765, pl.5, Venetian Stoves

Fig. 20   W & J Welldon, 1765, pl.6, Philadelphia Stoves

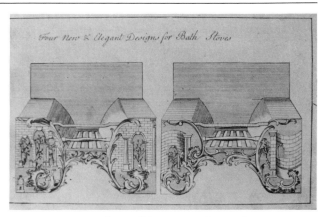

Fig. 21   W & J Welldon, 1765, pl.7, Bath Stoves

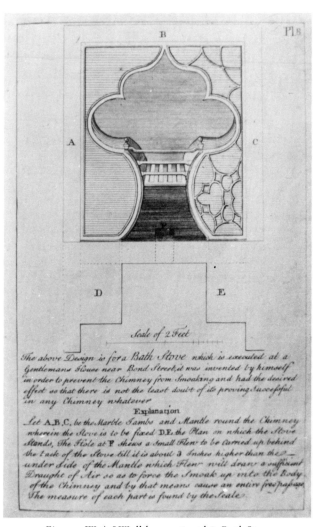

Fig. 22   W & J Welldon, 1765, pl.8, Bath Stove

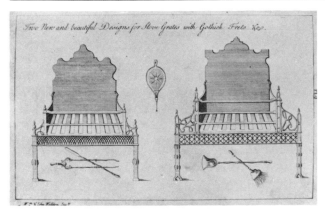

Fig. 23   W & J Welldon, 1765, pl.9, Stove Grates with
Gothick Frets

Fig. 27   W & J Welldon, 1765, pl.13, Gothic Stoves

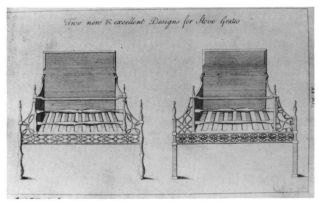

Fig. 24   W & J Welldon, 1765, pl.10, Stove Grates

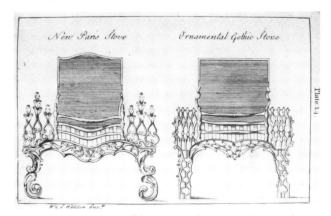

Fig. 28   W & J Welldon, 1765, pl.14, Paris Stove and
Gothic Stove

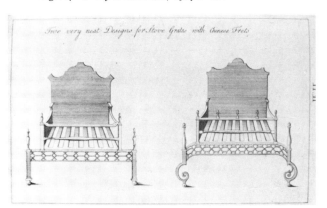

Fig. 25   W & J Welldon, 1765, pl.11, Stove Grates with
Chinese Frets

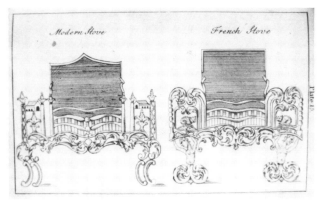

Fig. 29   W & J Welldon, 1765, pl.15, Modern Stove and
French Stove

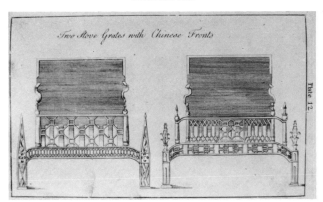

Fig. 26   W & J Welldon, 1765, pl.12, Stove Grates with
Chinese Fronts

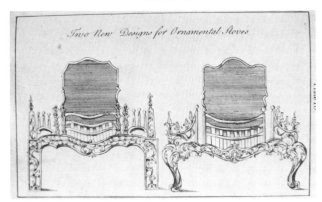

Fig. 30   W & J Welldon, 1765, pl.16, Ornamental Stoves

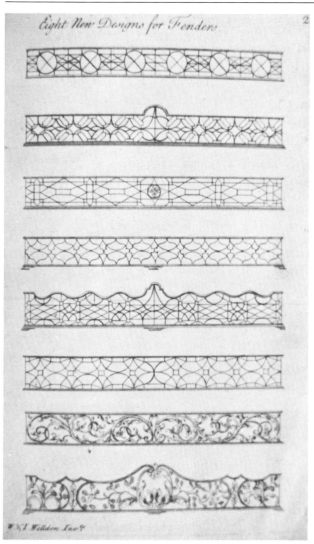

Fig. 31   *W & J Welldon, 1765, pl.21, Designs for Fenders*

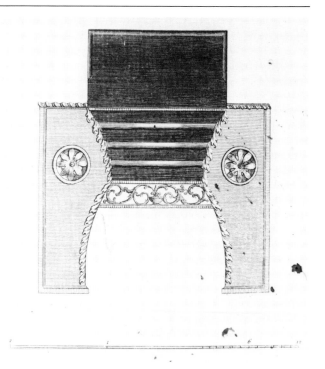

Fig. 33   *W. Glossop, 1771, pl.2*

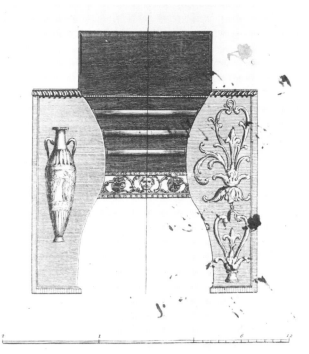

Fig. 32   *W. Glossop, 1771, pl.1*

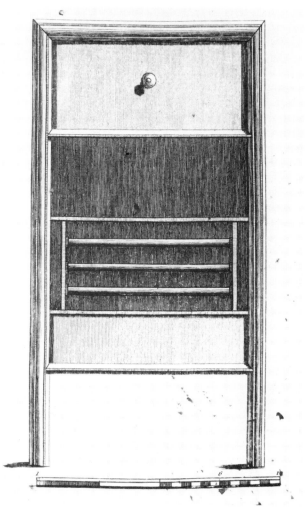

Fig. 34   *W. Glossop, 1771, pl.3*

In 1771 I. Taylor published *The Stove-Grate Makers Assistant* by W. Glossop which is also reprinted here (Figs 32–55) (from a copy in Bath Reference Library). The title-page is as follows:

THE

STOVE-GRATE MAKERS

ASSISTANT,

a TREASURY of

Original and Fashionable Designs

FOR

BATH STOVES, PENSYLVANIA STOVES,

Single & Double

STANDARD GRATES, FRETS &c

BY

W. GLOSSOP, Stove Grate Maker

Elegantly Engraved on Twenty-four Plates

Price 5s

LONDON

Published according to Act of Parliament Feb. 1st. 1771
by I. Taylor, at the Bible & Crown in Holborn
near Chancery Lane

The next significant body of pictorial source material associated with working smiths and founders is in the extensive Carron Company archive. This visual evidence, consisting of two drawing books dating from the late

18th and early 19th centuries, together with a printed catalogue of 1824 is considered in a separate section, pp. 66–69.

The earliest trade catalogue issued by a founder to assist retailers in ordering wares was apparently produced by Skidmore in 1811 (V & A Library 204.B.27). It

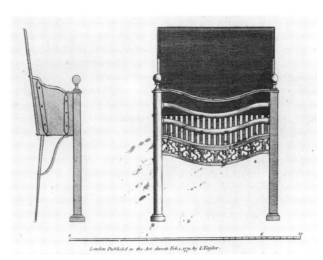

Fig. 36 W. Glossop, 1771, pl. 5

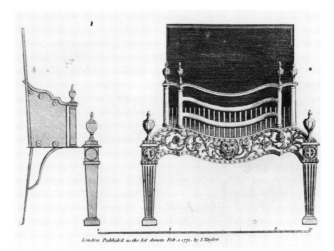

Fig. 37 W. Glossop, 1771, pl. 6

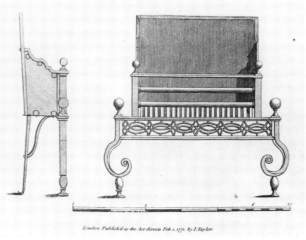

Fig. 38 W. Glossop, 1771, pl. 7

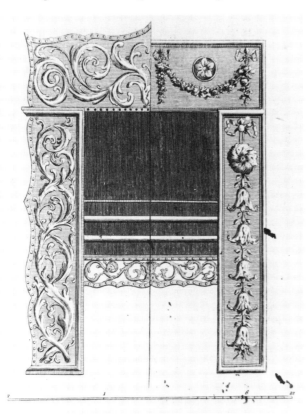

Fig. 35 W. Glossop, 1771, pl. 4

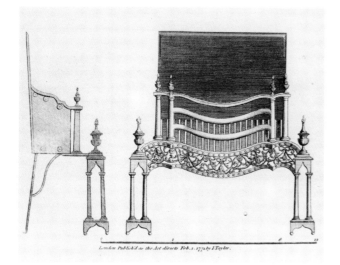

Fig. 39 W. Glossop, 1771, pl.8

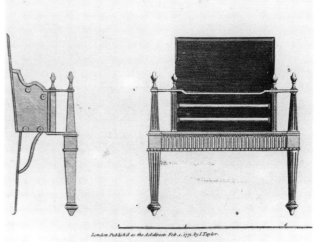

Fig. 42 W. Glossop, 1771, pl.11

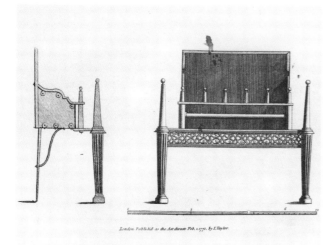

Fig. 40 W. Glossop, 1771, pl.9

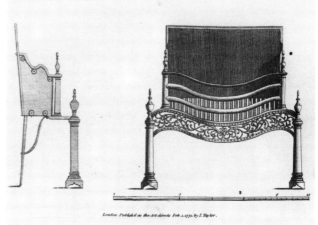

Fig. 43 W. Glossop, 1771, pl.12

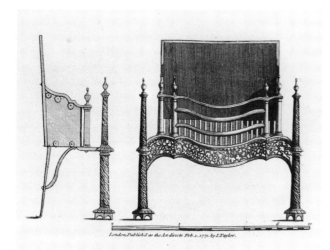

Fig. 41 W. Glossop, 1771, pl.10

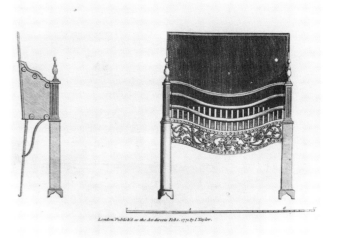

Fig. 44 W. Glossop, 1771, pl.13

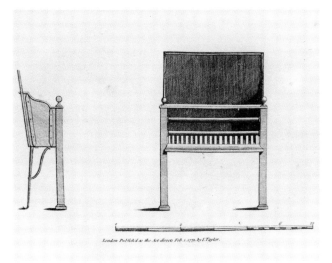

Fig. 45 W. Glossop, 1771, pl.14

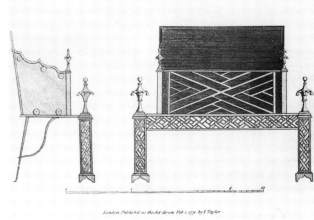

Fig. 48 W. Glossop, 1771, pl.17

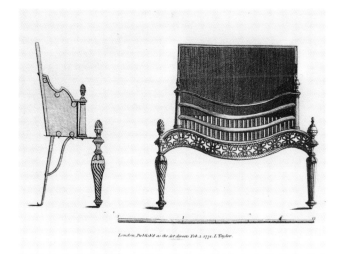

Fig. 46 W. Glossop, 1771, pl.15

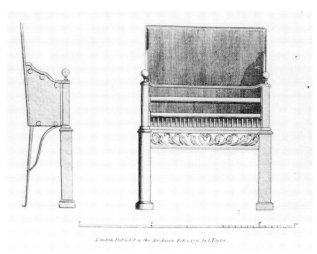

Fig. 49 W. Glossop, 1771, pl.18

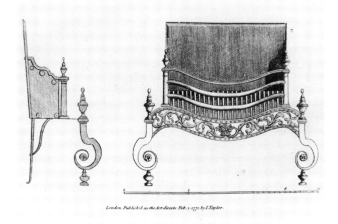

Fig. 47 W. Glossop, 1771, pl.16

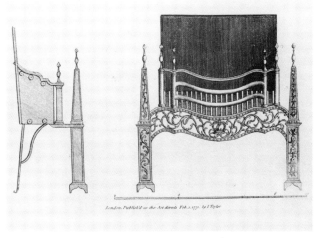

Fig. 50 W. Glossop, 1771, pl.19

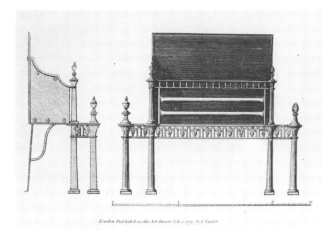

Fig. 51 W. Glossop, 1771, pl.20

Fig. 54 W. Glossop, 1771, pl.23

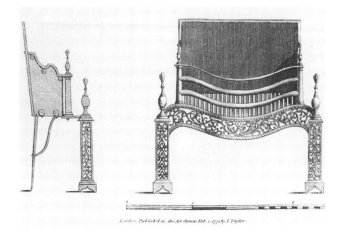

Fig. 52 W. Glossop, 1771, pl.21

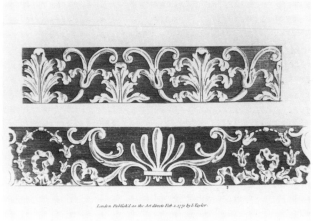

Fig. 55 W. Glossop, 1771, pl.24

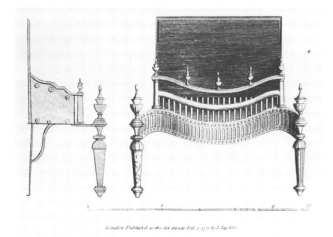

Fig. 53 W. Glossop, 1771, pl.22

is titled DESIGNS OF | STOVES, RANGES, VIRANDAS, RAILINGS, BELCONETS, &c | Including | The antique, Sarcophagus, Vause, Oval, | Gothic and Egyptian | BY | M & G Skidmore | FOUNDERS & STOVE GRATE | MANUFACTURERS, | No. 123, High Holborn; and 15, Coppice Row | CLERKENWELL'. The firm hoped 'The great Utility of this Work will appear most obvious

to everyone, more particularly to Country-Ironmongers', and still more so to the 'Residents of Ireland and Scotland — to those whose Premises or Capital will not permit them to keep a Stock on Hand, and who are not willing to risk the Fluctuation of Patterns ...'. The volume contains 85 designs for grates, stoves and ranges with a descriptive catalogue which is a mine of information about contemporary terminology for various design types (Fig. 11). The example of this London firm was followed in the 1820s by Messrs Longden, Walker & Co. of the Phoenix Foundary, Sheffield who published a pattern book illustrating cast-iron grates and Birmingham foundries soon followed their example. There is also at the Castle Museum, York a manuscript design book of c. 1836 which includes fireplaces and grates by W. Tomlinson-Walker of the Victoria Ironworks, York.

During the late-Regency period certain enterprising authors produced general works on the decorative arts. L. N. Cottingham's *The Smith and Founder's Director*, 1824 included a few stoves, fenders and grates, but the most impressive compendium covering all aspects of domestic interiors was J. C. Loudon's massive *Encyclopedia of Cottage, Farm and Villa Architecture and Furniture*, 1833 which went through ten editions. It describes in detail various types of kitchen ranges, warming stoves, early central heating systems and modern improved grates. Loudon was more interested in technology and the efficient use of fuel than style which gives an interesting slant to his often rather long-winded text. He warmly recommended Mr Sylvester's central heating system as 'one of the most powerful' and praised Nott's enclosed coal burning stove; Moser's open fireplace was considered 'one of the best that has been invented' owing to the fire chamber being formed of fireclay which absorbs and radiates heat more effectively than popular cast-iron grates. Sylvester's fireplace was said to 'exhibit the last great improvement in the mode of generating heat'. It had no fender, the hearth being composed of a fan-like bed of radiating spokes which extended into the bottom of the grate with an ashpit below. The library of Broughton Hall, Yorkshire, preserves a fine Sylvester fireplace.

DESIGNS BY FURNITURE MAKERS

In 1758 Thomas Johnson, a carver by trade, published an untitled collection of designs which included two chimneypieces featuring very ambitious rococo/gothic grates in the fireplace; two others show ostentatious gilt flower vases on the hearth. They are essentially 'stage props' for the elaborately carved chimneypieces and overmantels but one of the decorative vases may be the source of a painted chimney board (Cat. 56).

The third edition of Chippendale's *Director*, 1762 portrayed eight designs for stove grates in the rococo and gothic tastes, a ninth figures in his engraving for a chimneypiece. In the prefatory note it states 'I would recommend the ornamental Parts to be of wrought Brass, and as they may be made to take off, will be easily cleaned'. He never invoiced grates, fenders or fire irons to his customers and examples corresponding to his published designs are invariably Victorian in date.

In 1759 the cabinetmakers William Ince and John Mayhew announced the publication in weekly numbers of a collection of designs for furniture. They quickly ran into difficulties and in 1762 the incomplete series was issued as a volume titled *The Universal System of Household Furniture*. Three of the plates portraying chimneypieces show grates or andirons on the hearth, there are two designs for elaborate 'Venetian Stoves' in a flamboyant rococo style, five illustrations of 'Stove Grates', one 'Bath Stove', four patterns for fenders and four different fire dogs.

A rather pedestrian anthology of designs brought out by the opportunist print seller Robert Sayer *Houshold Furniture in Genteel Taste* went through four editions between 1759 and 64. The section devoted to ornamental ironwork illustrates twelve patterns for fenders, six andirons and two fire grates showing alternative treatments in a single plate. Elsewhere two engravings of chimneypieces illustrate stove grates. None of the designs by Johnson, Chippendale, Ince & Mayhew or in Sayer's collection are reproduced here because these pattern books are readily available in facsimile editions.

The extensive portfolio of drawings by John Linnell, cabinet maker, in the V & A include 19 for neoclassical grates, many of the sheets also bear sketches for grates on the verso (E. 373–89–1929). They appear to date from *c*. 1790–93, many being very showy, ornamented with circular fire backs, human figures, fabulous beasts and tripod motifs. Two are annotated 'Uxbridge House', one is inscribed 'for Duke of Queensbury' and many combine alternative treatments in a single drawing.

DESIGNS BY ARCHITECTS

This class of material falls naturally into two sections — manuscript and printed designs, and the following paragraphs mention a few of these sources. In 1754 Matthias Darly, architect and his collaborator George Edwards produced *A New Book of Chinese Designs*. The single plate (Fig. 56) devoted to chimney furniture shows a basket grate, footman, bellows, set of fire irons and a hearth brush in a predictably exotic style. Although rather fanciful this is a significant record.

The designs which John Carter, architect, contributed to the *Builder's Magazine*, issued monthly between 1774 and 78 included several for decorative grates in an over-elaborate neoclassical style. While interesting as specimens of taste it is doubtful if any of his highly wrought designs were actually carried out.

Rudolph Ackermann's *The Repository of Arts* which appeared in monthly numbers between 1809 and 1828, included plates of fashionable furniture and interiors. These have recently been collected together and published as a single volume. Illustrations of chimneypieces, fire grates and accessories contributed by the Pugins, George Bullock and others appeared in December 1813; January and October 1816; June 1817; November 1821; December 1822; June and December 1825; September 1827 and July 1828.

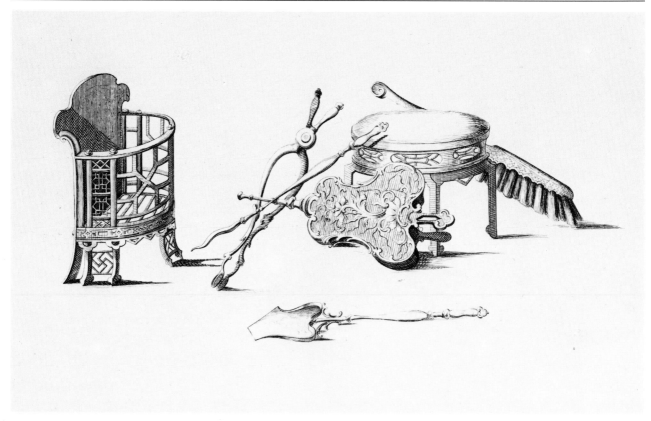

Fig. 56   M. Darly and G. Edwards, 'A New Book of Chinese Designs', 1754, pl.64

Richard Bridgens' *Designs for Furniture with Candelabra and Interior Decoration*, 1838, devoted three plates to chimneypieces, grates and fenders. The origins of his antiquarian style can be traced back to designs which he executed for James Watt at Aston Hall *c.* 1819–25 (Cat. 15).

Robert Adam was renowned for creating unified room schemes, hence it is only to be expected that his voluminous drawings in the Sir John Soane's Museum contain many designs for chimneypieces, grates and even chimney boards while others survive in country house archives (Cat. 9). Since Adam charged his clients for drawings many are beautifully coloured and finely detailed. The majority are preserved in three volumes: XVII, fols 120–39 (including a particularly elegant series for Sir Watkin Williams-Wynn's house at 20 St James Square); XXIV, fols 55, 71, 155–58, 160, 196–99, 205, 208–09, 211–13, 216–19, 221; and LVI, fols 11–12, 14, 48. Little is at present known about the identity of the founders commissioned to execute Adam's grates, but in 1773–74 Hopkins & Co. supplied stove grates, fenders and fire irons to Sir Watkin Williams-Wynn including one for the front drawing room with '4 round fluted term feet with rams heads on Do, the whole to Mr Adams Designs and Curiously embosed' (Nat. Lib. of Wales,

Wynnstay MS, Box 115/17). A superb paktong grate and fender from the Gallery at Croome Court, corresponding to a design dated 1765, for which Adam charged £5 5s od was sold last year by Crowthers, Ltd to a private collector. It may relate to payments in Hartley & Cooper's bill of 16 June 1766 for smith's work for the Earl of Coventry 'by Order of Robert Adam Esq.' for which they received £55 4s 4d. This paucity of documentary information in a well-researched career underlines how little is at present known about who was supplying chimney furniture for smart neoclassical interiors.

There can be little doubt that a systematic study of country house archives will eventually answer a number of questions. Two isolated references noted by my colleague Terry Friedman indicate the kind of evidence awaiting discovery. John Vardy's account in the Hackwood papers (Hants. RO 11M 49) records under March 1763 'Drawing for the 2 large Grates in the Great Room, attending and Directing Mr Chamberlain about the same £2 2s od'; while the Fitzwilliam papers (Northants. RO Milton 86) contain two elegant anonymous drawings of 1750 for a dining room grate. Our section on tradesmen's bills pp. 70–71 identifies a few London and provincial founders supplying stove grates.

STOVE GRATE MAKERS

It is clear that chimney furniture was an expensive element in fashionable interiors, grates were often designed by leading architects and made an important contribution to room schemes, yet little is known about the identity of the leading smiths and founders. A trawl of most estate archives generally produces a scattering of bills from or payments to ironmongers and smiths for grates and fire accessories, although it is not always easy to discover if they made or merely supplied the goods as agents. The Petworth papers, for example, contain an invoice of 1778–79 from Alexander Brodie, patent stove maker (PHA 6611) and another from Richard Norris (1764) listing 4 stove grates and a fender for Egremont House, London (PHA 6615). These items have not been identified, but the ironmongers Bickley & Lardner supplied a polished steel grate and fender which survive for the Yellow Drawing Room at Wimpole created by Soane in the 1790s.

Thomas Blockley (1705–89) of Birmingham who specialized in high quality locks, brass door furniture and other sorts of hardware fitments also occasionally invoiced chimney furniture. In 1757 he provided a polished grate and fender for Holkham and the Bowood papers record under March 1768 a payment to him 'For a Stove Grate £17 0s 4d'.

The Earl of Dumfries employed two Edinburgh smiths when ordering hearth furniture for Dumfries House, Ayrshire. The principal rooms were equipped by David Robertson in 1760. He provided the Drawing Room with '1 fine pollish'd Grate with a fine fender & white iron sole, a back for the Grate & fire tongs and poker £20'. Robertson in fact furnished 17 fireplaces at a cost of £114 18s 8d. The lesser rooms were entrusted to John Richardson, smith of Edinburgh. It is noteworthy that both tradesmen were only required to supply pokers and tongs, there are no references to fire shovels.

William Aislaby of Studley Royal in Yorkshire purchased three grates 'one steel wiear finder' two sets of 'fiear shovel & Tongs' and a 'moulded finder in frett work' from Peter Thornhill of Darlington, Co. Durham in 1749. In December 1754 he obliged his patron by sending a copy of 'Chippendale's Book', published earlier that year, when he despatched a fender and set of fire irons (Leeds Archives Dept VR 286, Bundle B, pt 1). It is fairly easy, given time, to trace relevant documentation in country house archives and such evidence, as it accumulates, is obviously of value, but more can be gained from studying the commissions of a single firm.

Maurice Tobin, whitesmith and ironmonger of Briggate in Leeds, remains a shadowy figure, but his obituary in 1773 described him as 'the most eminent in his profession of any in the North of England' and what is known of his activities confirms this reputation. The fullest account of Tobin's career 'The Kirklees Iron Bridge of 1769 and its Builder' by David Nortcliffe (YAS Industrial History Section) 1979 concentrates on the 'most curious bridge of one arch, six feet wide, and 72 feet in span; made entirely of iron' which he constructed for Sir George Armytage at Kirklees Hall, in 1769 — that is ten years before the Shropshire iron bridge was opened. Tobin often worked in association with John Carr and later Robert Adam at houses such as Aske Hall, Harewood, Fairfax House, York, Campsall Hall, near Doncaster, Temple Newsam, Newby Hall, Serlby, Wentworth Woodhouse, Thoresby and Heaton Hall. After his death aged seventy in 1773 his son Henry took over for a year before selling the business to John Rodgers.

In the course of field work, Newby Hall has emerged as the key house for the study of Tobin's chimney furniture. The bright steel stove grate in the Tapestry Room, designed by Adam and furnished by Chippendale between about 1769 and 73 bears an inscription 'TOBIN LEEDS | 1522' (Cat. 7) while another impressive grate in the dining room (Cat. 6) is also signed '[MAU]RICE T [OBIN] LEEDS'. Furthermore, the collection at Newby also includes two superlative steel fenders boldly stamped 'RODGERS LEEDS' (Cats 17 and 18). These are so far the only recorded items bearing the name of Tobin or his successor, but an inventory of furniture at Serlby Hall, Notts., taken in 1774 lists in the Dining Room 'Grate (M. Tobin) Leeds' and in the Drawing Room 'Range (maker Morice Tobin Leeds)' which suggest that they, too, were signed.

Surviving documents show that Maurice Tobin often supplied railings, gates, staircase balustrades and other ornamental cast-iron work besides chimney furniture and a wide range of domestic hardware. In January 1765 he wrote from Leeds to Baca Franks of Campsall Hall 'I have sent by the London waggon to be left at Robin Hood well the Balustrades for ye stair case &c and I sent ye week before two fenders, 3 setts of Tong and 1 spring for ye Door next the yard, which hope will arrive safe & please, ye Ballastrades &c are in two Hampers & a Bundle, please to sett them in a dry place, & not to unpack them, afraid anything be lost, when it is convenient shall wait on you to putt them up, ye grate for the Dineing room the Holidays prevented being finish'd as my men did not work any, but shall be now finish'd with all expedition.

1765		£	s	d
Jan 5	2 Open Chince fenders	2	5	0
	1 sett of Fire Shovel & Tongs		9	0
	1 Sett of Ditto		8	0
	1 Sett of Ditto		7	0'

On 12 February he wrote again to Franks: 'I sent you by the London waggons, 1 Grate 1 fender, 1 Sett of Tongs & 1 Hearth Brush for the Dineing Room, 1 Grate & 1 Sett of Tongs & hearth Brush for the Breakfast Room, &

3 Cast Iron stoves with grates, bush plates & covers, 1 Cast Oven, Cast Shelf & plate shelf, Damper, 10 Barrs for the grates, 1 Mouth cole rake & Shovell . . . the fender for the Dressing Room will be sent in a Short time'. The letter suggests most items were bespoke rather than taken from stock.

Two bills from the Harewood papers illuminate the scope of Tobin's trade. The earliest, dated 1757–58 invoices a wide variety of goods ranging from hinges, locks, brass knobs, handles, escutcheons, bolts, pulleys, curtain rings and screws to kitchen candlesticks, shreding knives, a bell system and cole skepts. It is worth extracting the entries relating to grates, etc. since this kind of documentation is seldom published. Some of the items are given pattern numbers and others were priced according to weight.

1757		£	s	d
Feb 24	1 Cast stove plate & Cover			
	130 at 2d	1	1	0
Aug 23	1 Gilt Hearth Brush		1	4
	1 Wallnut Do		1	3
	1 Painted Do			10
25	3 X-ranges 59½ at 5	1	4	9
Sep 14	1 Bright Grate with Common-ribbon apron to Sett in stone	1	0	0
1758				
June 6	1 flatt Obelisk Grate with Scrowl & Leafe apron No. 877	5	5	0
20	1 Bright Round Grate to Sett in stone with Common Ribbon apron		15	0
July 2	2 Setts of tongs	1	6	0
	1 fender for the Drawing Room	1	17	0
8	a new fire Shovel & poaker 14 lb at 6		7	0
24	1 Long Gothick fender	1	1	0
	1 Round plain fender for ye Butlers pantery		7	6
	1 Sett of tongs		7	0

A substantial bill of 1772–73 from Henry Tobin to Edwin Lascelles of Harewood, totalling £387 15s 3d. contains a similar repertoire, although it also includes several heavy items such as two pairs of 'large Iron Gates £60 2s 6d' and '12 dorick Columns ornamented with flower pott Balls & flaming tops £68 3s 4d'. The descriptions of chimney furniture are instructive for their use of contemporary terminology. It is unfortunate that all the grates at Harewood were replaced by often ostentatiously splendid Victorian specimens, although a large collection of Adam period fire irons and fenders

survive in attic stores. Only one set of fire irons, those with 'flaming' tops' made in 1772 for the saloon can be confidently identified (Cat. 30).

1772		£	s	d
Ap. 4	1 New Bath Stove, the Apron ornamented with gothick Curves & flower de luce & a gothick flower in the centre for the ante Chamber			
	1 Ditto ornamented with diamonds & gothick Curves for Mr Lascelles Room	7	10	0
	1 Ditto ornamented with a Chinese Apron & a shell in the Center for the Chinese dressing Room			
15	1 Grated case hardened fire shovel for Lady Flemings ante-Chamber		7	0
17	1 Stand Grate No — , 22 in back high pedestals, Chinese Feet & square chinese obelisks with flower potts upon ditto, a Streight front with a Scallop'd Chinese frett Apron a gudround & 2 gudround Cups for the Octagon Room	24	0	0
June 9	8 Polish'd Balls for rais'g ye feet of a round obelisk grate with gudround caps & flamin'g Balls & pollis'g do		18	0
26	2 Inside Grates for the Grates in the Salloon	1	0	0
	2 pr of Tongs & 2 Pokers, case hardened with flaming tops for the Salloon	3	12	0
	1 Sett of Tongs with a grated fire shovel for ye Hall		18	0
	6 cast backs for Grates	5	7	7
29	Cleaning & polish'g Grates at Harewood house 4 men 20 days	2	10	0
Aug 31	2 Engraved Fenders for the Salloon	10	10	0
1773				
July 20	1 pine for a stove in the Sub Hall		12	0

The reference to a stove calls to mind the first entry under 30 December 1772 in the surviving portion of Chippendale's Harewood account 'A Pattern for a Pyramid Stove with Antique Ornaments Carved in Mahogany — to Cast from £22'. This strongly suggests that Chippendale designed and carved the wooden models for an unknown smith to cast the decorative elements of a spectacular hot-air stove.

ABRAHAM BUZAGLO
1716–88

This account of Buzaglo's colourful career and his spectacular 'warming machines' is based largely on material from rather inaccessible learned journals which Claude Blair has kindly made available, together with the contents of research files assembled by Graham Hood and his colleagues at the Colonial Williamsburg Foundation. Abraham Buzaglo was a Moroccan Jew who settled in England in 1762, becoming naturalized in 1771. The climatic shock appears to have stirred an inventive streak in his personality for he spent the remainder of his life patenting heating devices and experimenting with cures for the gout. On 25 April 1765 he registered a 'New machine for warming rooms of all sizes with a coal fire'; in 1769 he patented a gadget for 'warming the feet of persons riding in carriages' and in 1779 took out another pertaining to 'instruments for exercise' to relieve the gout. His obsession became something of a national joke, being lampooned in verse and ridiculed in caricatures, even Horace Walpole made fun of him. However, despite this playful mockery Buzaglo is, today, an important figure for anyone interested in historic heating appliances. He created two of the most spectacular 18th century enclosed stoves to have survived — one expressing a flamboyant rococo character, the other in an orderly neoclassical style; a single signed stove plate dated 1765 is also extant (*Rococo*, exh. cat., V & A, 1984, K5, repr.).

Certainly the best known specimen of Buzaglo's work is the 'Treble Tier Patent Warming Machine' made in London in 1770 and presented to the first Virginia House of Burgesses (Fig. 57). This has been admired by millions of visitors to Colonial Williamsburg and is impressively documented in the Virginia State Library Archives (Botetourt papers L33–503 and 50–1) and the Badminton muniments. On 15th August 1770 Buzaglo boasted in a letter to Lord Botetourt, Governor of Virginia, who had ordered the stove 'that cost nor trouble was spared in the execution; The Elegence of workmanship and Impression of every particular joint, does honour to Great Britain, it excels in grandeur anything ever seen of the kind, and is a Master piece not to be equalled in all Europe, it has met with General Applause, and could not be sufficiently admired'. The stove is indeed a *tour de force*, an enviable status symbol, and although apparently missing its topmost stage, has, until now amply secured its makers reputation. The original bill recently discovered by Graham Hood at Badminton (together with the bill for two others commissioned for the Governor's Palace) records that, including the expenses of packing, transport and various extras the cost amounted to £143 13s 3d. A precise set of instructions for using Buzaglo's 'apparatus' also survives together with the original patent specification (Williamsburg files).

Fig. 57 Treble Tier Patent Warming Machine made by Abraham Buzaglo in 1770 for the Virginia House of Representatives.

The Colonial Williamsburg Foundation

A second magnificent three tier cast-iron stove is preserved at Knole Park, Kent, signed and dated 'BUZAGLO 1774' (Fig. 58). It is visible in Victorian photographs stationed in the centre of the great hall but

Fig. 58 Treble Tier Patent Warming Machine by Abraham Buzaglo, 1774.

The National Trust, Knole

thankfully was removed when obsolete to the orangery rather than being scrapped. Its countenance, in contrast to the rococo exuberance of the Williamsburg model (1770) is invested with a robust system of neoclassical ornament. Students of decorative cast-iron work are indeed fortunate to have two such splendid signed, dated and provenanced specimens to study.

A note titled 'Hot Air from Cambridge' contributed by J. C. T. Oates to *The Library*, 18 (1963), pp. 140–42 describes a Buzaglo stove installed in the Divinity School at Cambridge in 1774. It disappeared long ago, but the associated documentation consisting of Buzaglo's trade card (Fig. 59), his printed bill-head and the original receipt is of capital interest (CU Archives VCV 23/1). The trade card, decorated with six stove patterns, gives his address as 'facing Somerset House, Strand' and the printed bill lists eleven different models in production: 'A Short Pyramid Patent Warming Machine | A Long Pyramid | A First Size Pyramid | A Royal Pyramid | A Small Single Tier | A Large Single Tier | A Small Double Tier | a Large Double Tier | A Treble Tier | A Laundry | A. Butlers'. A large double tier was purchased for the Divinity School costing 15 gns, an extra 40 ft of funnel, carriage charges at 4*d* per mile, the expence of installation, etc brought the total to £31 16*s* 8*d*. The account was receipted by 'Jacob Buzaglo Junr'.

The closely printed trade card claimed that Buzaglo's machines 'surpass in Utility, Beauty and Goodness anything hitherto Invented in all Europe'; they not only 'cast an equal & agreeable Heat to any Part of the Room, and are not attended by any Stench', but also contain 'a neat Oven to bake Puddings, Cakes, Tarts or Custards, & a bright Fire to be seen at Pleasure': they 'preserve the Ladies Complexions and Eye Sight' and 'warm equally the whole Body, without scorching the Face or Legs'; they possess 'other Advantages too tedious to insert'; and were also recommended to 'Silk Throwsters, Callico Printers, Master Taylors & other Shops' and to 'Gentlemen concerned in new Buildings'.

There must be many so far unrecorded archive references to Buzaglo. One of his cast-iron 'fire machines' given by the headmaster Dr Wharton to Winchester College Library in 1772 is briefly mentioned in *The Library*, 17 (1962), p. 27 and Cyril Staal has drawn my attention to an entry in the pocket account book of John Parker of Saltram recording that 'Buzaglo' was paid £12 11*s* 10*d* in 1771. When he died in 1788 a brief obituary appeared in the *Gentleman's Magazine* 'Aged 72, Mr Abraham Buzaglo, of Dean-street Soho, inventor of the stove called after his name, which he afterwards applied as a cure for the gout, and wherein he has been so much exceeded by the late Mr Sharp'.

Literature: C. Roth, 'The Amazing Clan of Buzaglo', *Transactions of the Jewish Historical Society of England*, XXIII (1971), pp. 11–21.

Fig. 59 Abraham Buzaglo's Trade Card, 1774.

Cambridge University Archives

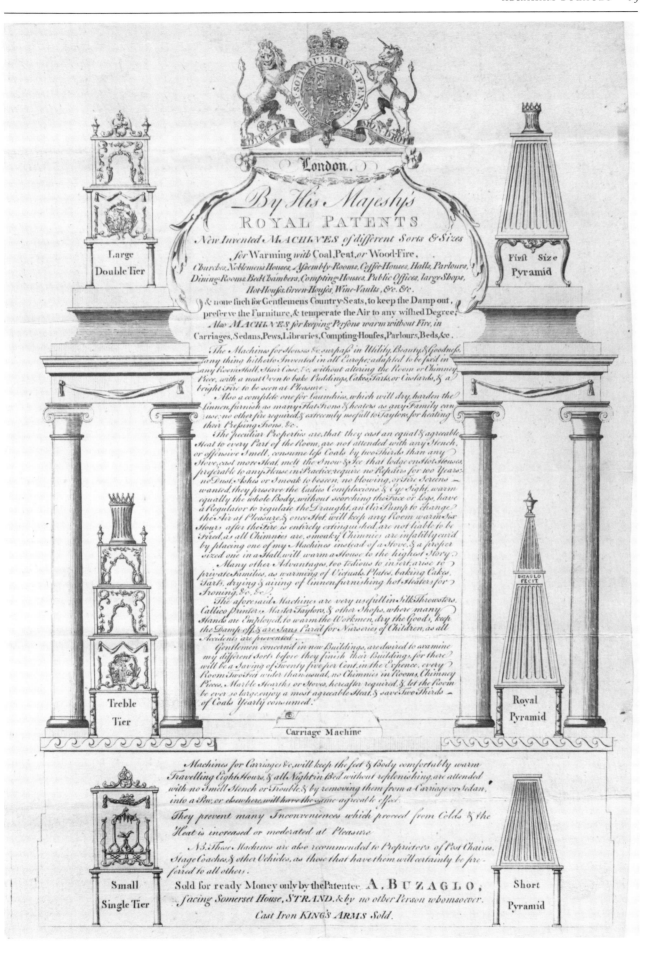

London.

By His Majesty's
ROYAL PATENTS

New Invented MACHINES of different Sorts & Sizes
for Warming with Coal, Peat, or Wood-Fire,
Churches, Noblemens Houses, Assembly-Rooms, Coffee-Houses, Halls, Parlours,
Dining-Rooms, Bed Chambers, Compting-Houses, Public Offices, large Shops,
Hot-Houses, Green-Houses, Wine-Vaults, &c. &c.
& none such for Gentlemens Country-Seats, to keep the Damp out,
preserve the Furniture, & temperate the Air to any wished Degree;
Also MACHINES for keeping Persons warm without Fire, in
Carriages, Sedans, Pews, Libraries, Compting-Houses, Parlours, Beds &c.

The Machines for Houses &c. surpass in Utility, Beauty & Goodness,
any thing hitherto Invented in all Europe; adapted to be fixd in
any Room, Hall, Stair Case, &c. without altering the Room or Chimney
Piece, with a neat Oven to bake Puddings, Cakes, Tarts, or Custards, & a
bright Fire to be seen at Pleasure.

Also a complete one for Laundries, which will dry, harden the
Linnen, furnish as many Flat-Irons & heaters as any Family can
use; no other fire required, & extreemly usefull to Taylors for heating
their Pressing Irons, &c.

The peculiar Properties are, that they cast an equal & agreeable
Heat to every Part of the Room, are not attended with any Stench,
or offensive Smell, consume less Coals by two thirds than any
Stove, cast more Heat, melt the Snow & Ice that lodge on Hot-Houses,
preferable to any House in Practice; require no Repairs for two Years;
no Dust, Ashes or Smoak to be seen, no blowing, or Fire Screens
wanted, they preserve the Ladies Complexions & Eye Sight, warm
equally the whole Body, without scorching the Face or Legs, have
a Regulator to regulate the Draught, an Air Pump to change
the Air at Pleasure, & once Hot, will keep any Room warm six
Hours after the Fire is entirely extinguished, are not liable to be
Fired, as all Chimnies are, smoaky Chimnies are infalibly curd
by placing one of my Machines instead of a Stove, & a proper
sized one in a Hall, will warm a House to the highest Story.

Many other Advantages, too tedious to insert, arise to
private Families, as warming of Victuals, Plates, baking Cakes,
Tarts, drying & airing of Linnen, furnishing hot Heaters for
Ironing, &c. &c.

The aforesaid Machines are very usefull in Silk-Throwsters,
Callico Printers, Master Taylors, & other Shops, where many
Hands are Employed, to warm the Workmen, dry the Goods, keep
the Damp off, & are Sans Pareil for Nurseries of Children, as all
Accidents are prevented.

Gentlemen concernd in new Buildings, are desired to examine
my different Sorts before they finish their Buildings, for there
will be a Saving of Twenty five per Cent. in the Expence, every
Room Two feet wider than usual, no Chimnies in Rooms, Chimney
Pieces, Marble Hearths or Stoves, hereafter required, & let the Room
be ever so large, enjoy a most agreeable Heat, & save Two Thirds
of Coals Yearly consumed.

Large
Double Tier

First Size
Pyramid

Treble
Tier

Royal
Pyramid

Carriage Machine

Machines for Carriages &c. will keep the feet & Body comfortably warm
Travelling Eight Hours, & all Night in Bed without replenishing, are attended
with no Smell, Stench or Trouble, & by removing them from a Carriage or Sedan,
into a Pew, or elsewhere, will have the same agreeable Effect.

They prevent many Inconveniences which proceed from Colds & the
Heat is increased or moderated at Pleasure.

N.B. These Machines are also recommended to Proprietors of Post Chaises,
Stage Coaches, & other Vehicles, as those that have them will certainly be preferred to all others.

Sold for ready Money only by the Patentee A. BUZAGLO,
facing Somerset House, STRAND, & by no other Person whomsoever.

Cast Iron KING'S ARMS Sold.

Small
Single Tier

Short
Pyramid

CARRON IRON COMPANY AND THE COALBROOKDALE COMPANY

In 1759 the Carron Co. was founded near Falkirk, Stirlingshire by John Roebuck, Samuel Garbett and William Cadell, their intention being to make the company a major iron-producing firm. When Thomas Pennant visited the works in 1769 he described the concern as 'the greatest of the kind in *Europe* . . . Above 1,200 men are employed. Cannon and all kinds of castings produced'. Making stoves and grates (Cat. 13) soon became an important branch once the Adam brothers were enlisted to provide a variety of ornamental patterns; designs were also supplied internally by William and Henry Haworth for hob grate panels, etc. This specialist line was not without its problems: it proved expensive to carve intricate models and although Carron's light castings used a high phosphorous iron capable of reproducing delicate designs the reliefs were not always satisfactory. In 1772 the management requested 'Messrs Adams to send a pattern more simple and the figures more strongly impressed'. Every effort was made to procure 'new and fanciful elegant patterns' because it was felt 'the appearance and neatness will give a great preference at market to any in London . . . and will be a means of keeping up the price'. Agents in London were urged to send artistic plaster of Paris figures suitable for decorative castings, which should exhibit 'Light and Expressive and Graceful Attitudes and be not too much charged with Drapery and Ornament'.

Ian Gow has observed privately that although present day scholars tend to think of the Carron Co. as an art manufactory at the Adams' beck and call there is very little evidence in their spectacularly complete archive (at the Scottish Record Office) to support this claim. What the firm was really interested in was mass production of articles like pipes, guns and implements. Fire grates and stoves suited this policy because they could be produced by the thousand. Much of the designing was done by the resident Haworths who appear to have been more interested in the limitations imposed by casting methods and the reaction of the mass market than aesthetics. There is little evidence of them striving to match their technique to the intended design, rather they usually preferred to modify the drawing. Because their ordinance branch brought them into contact with politicians they would sometimes oblige an influential figure with something out of the normal run but on the whole, when anyone asked for something special (as when the Edinburgh Assembly Rooms asked for 4 smaller than average stoves) the firm quoted a frighteningly high price for making a 'pattern' and drove the point home by saying that they thought it unlikely that it would ever be used elsewhere.

Identifying extant Carron work from surviving documents rather than the patterns (many of which bear the firm's name on the plinth) is impossible because they tended to sell in bulk to agents, so the ultimate

Fig. 60 Pedestal Stove, attributed to the Carron Iron Co., c.1780, formerly at Compton Place, Sussex.

The Trustees of the Victoria & Albert Museum

Fig. 61 Carron Co., Pyramid Stove,
late 18th century, pen and ink.

Scottish Record Office

Fig. 62 Carron Co., Pedestal Stove,
late 18th century, pen and ink.

Scottish Record Office

Fig. 63 Carron Co., Pedestal Stove,
late 18th century, pen and ink.

Scottish Record Office

Fig. 64 Carron Co., Vase Stove, late
18th century, pen and ink.

Scottish Record Office

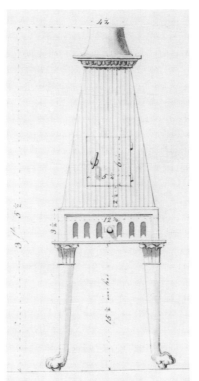

Fig. 65 Carron Co., Shop Stove, late
18th century, pen and ink.

Scottish Record Office

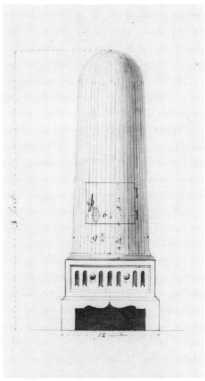

Fig. 66 Carron Co., Round fluted
Pillar Stove, late 18th century,
pen and ink.

Scottish Record Office

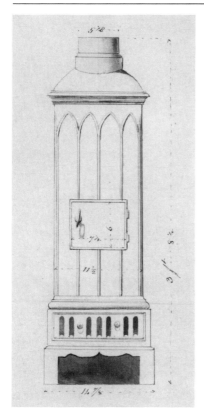

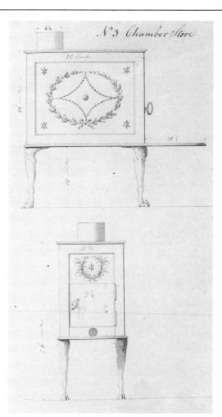

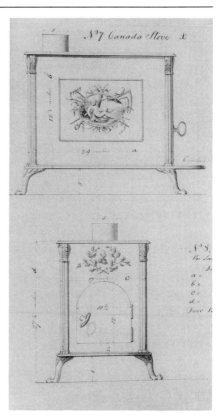

Fig. 67 Carron Co., Gothic Stove,
late 18th century, pen and ink.

Scottish Record Office

Fig. 68 Carron Co., Chamber Stove,
late 18th century, pen and ink.

Scottish Record Office

Fig. 69 Carron Co., Canada Stove,
late 18th century, pen and ink.

Scottish Record Office

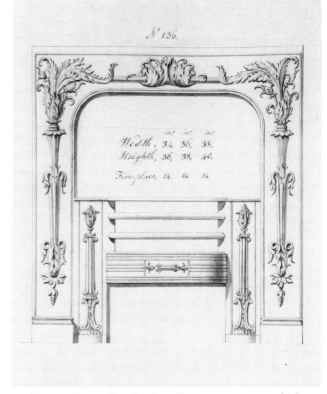

Fig. 70 Carron Co., Improved Stove, late 18th century,
pen and ink.

Scottish Record Office

Fig. 71 Carron Co., Register Grate c.1840, pen and ink.

Scottish Record Office

destination is never recorded. In view of their concentration on the mass market it is difficult to believe that they were responsible for such splendid work as the vase stoves at Kedleston, those in the sculpture gallery at Newby or the magnificent cast-iron chimneypiece in the dining room at Blair Adam, Kinross-shire for instance. However, a pedestal stove in the V & A (Fig. 60) is nearly enough related to extant drawings to permit an attribution to Carron. It is provenanced to Compton Place, Sussex and evidently dates from the period of Lord George Cavendish's refurnishing in the 1780s.

The Carron Co. business papers are rather weak on pictorial sources; however, the collection preserves two volumes of manuscript designs which feature neoclassical stoves and grates and a later printed catalogue. The most interesting from our point of view (GD 58/15/3) contains an anthology of finely detailed pen and grey wash drawings for cast-iron fireplace surrounds, hob grates, register stoves and various hot air stoves with fancy trade names. Many of these are very impressive and no apology is necessary for publishing a selection because they illustrate specimens of a branch of decorative cast-iron work that has all but totally disappeared (Figs 61–71). Many of these drawings are repeated in a small scrap book (GD 58/15/4) while the printed catalogue of 1824 includes less grand Improved Rumford, Half Register, Pantheon, Forest, Kentish Cottage, Gothic and Sussex Cottage 'duck's nest' grates.

Falkirk museum now houses the entire collections of the old Carron Co. museum which contains many castings for stove grates and examples of work designed by the Adam brothers and the Haworths. Most of this material is in store but the display includes a flamboyant rococo revival cast-iron fireplace signed and dated 'CARRON CO NOV 30th 1840'. Many other public and private collections such as Ironbridge and the Geffrye Museum possess signed grates.

The commercial success of the Carron ironworks caused many firms specializing in light castings to spring up in the neighbourhood, particulary during the period 1850–90, the two most important rivals established before 1840 being Abbot's Foundry Company (1804) and the Falkirk Iron Company (1819). The latter sometimes identified their work with a maker's name. The Falkirk museum contains a very extensive holding of local Victorian printed trade catalogues and drawings illustrating chimney furniture. The two earliest from the Falkirk Iron Co. date from about 1840. The collection also includes several interesting scrap books by Henry Hoole & Co. of Sheffield who executed designs for grates by Alfred Stevens before being taken over by the Falkirk Iron Co. The products of the iron founding industry in this area would repay detailed study.

COALBROOKDALE COMPANY

This famous ironworks, founded by the Darby family in the 17th century, earned a national reputation during the Georgian period for its wide range of domestic and constructional cast-iron products. Following the opening of the spectacular Iron Bridge spanning the Severn in 1779 the site became a popular tourist attraction and a detailed description of the works written by a visitor in 1801 contains a catalogue of 'the regular articles cast by the Coalbrook Dale Co.'. This list includes 'Chimney pieces of various sorts | Fenders of various patterns | Fire stands of various sorts | Grates in great variety | Hob registers | Kitchen grates in great variety | Pantheons in great variety | Pyramid Stoves of various sorts | Registers | Rumford stoves | Stoves of all sorts Bath, German'.

It is apparent that the Company's product range included manifold stoves, grates and associated chimney furniture; however, nothing is known about who was designing these wares during the pre-Victorian period. An article in the *Art Union* of August 1846 illustrates two of their ornamental grates, the earliest (undated) catalogue was apparently issued in the 1840s and their celebrated two volume catalogue appeared in 1875. Fortunately some products bear the firm's name 'C DALE' or 'DALE' so a census of signed examples could be attempted. In fact no such study has yet been undertaken. One of their most attractive patterns was a hob grate incorporating the Iron Bridge as part of the design (Cat. 12).

JUTSHAM'S CARLTON HOUSE DAYBOOK 1806–29

Geoffrey de Bellaigue with his customary generosity has very kindly provided copies of the relevant sections of the day book kept by Benjamin Jutsham in which are recorded the daily arrivals at Carlton House of works of art of all kinds between 1806 and 1829. The inventory, kept in the Lord Chamberlain's Office, St James's Palace, is of such exceptional interest that no excuse is needed for printing the following extract. Not only are the descriptions often very detailed but the names of suppliers are recorded.

FENDERS

MR HOPKINS, 1808

Two wire Fenders; Two sets of fire irons

A Circular wire Fender Steel rim painted green; a poker

A Circular Steel Fender and Set of Fire Irons

A Steel Fender

A Circular Steel Fender and Set of Fire Irons

MR FELTHAM, 1808

A Circular Steel Fender and Set of Fire Irons

MR MACNAUGHTON, 1809–11

A Gilt Fender; Fire Irons with Standards

Two handsome Plated Fenders and Two Fire Guards to Correspond

A Fender Steel Cut to the Above

A Fender, Fire Guard and Fire Irons to correspond with the Grate

MR FELTHAM, 1812

A Fender Painted Green. A Set of Fire Irons

CUTLER & MACNAUGHTON, 1812

Two handsome Small Bronze Metal Fenders with Brass mouldings &c.

MR BROWNLEY, 1813

A Steel Fender with Standards on Brass Balls

MR ALLDAY, 73 HIGH STREET BIRMINGHAM, 1820

A Large Brass Fender

FROM THE LORD CHAMBERLAIN'S OFFICE, 1827

A Large Polished Steel Fender with Cut Steel mouldings in Egg and Tongue, and Beads; Thrown into Three Pannels in Front, the Centre Pannel having a Rosett in Silver, enclosed by a wreath composed of the Rose, the Thistle and Shamrock in Gilt Metal. The Two End pannels are ornamented with The Royal Arms, in Gilt Metal, 5 Feet 6 inches Long. . . A Set of Polished Steel Fire Irons, ingraved with the Rose Garter & Crown — the Blade is perforated.

MR FELTHAM, 1811

A Steel Fender; a hanging Brass Fire Guard, A Set of Fire Irons.

FIRE GUARDS

MR HOPKINS, 1808–09

Three fire Guards to hang on the Grates made of Brass

A Folding wire Fire Guard painted Green

A Circular wire Fire Guard painted Green

A Brass Fire Guard to hang on the grate

A Fire Guard Circular painted Green

A Wire Fire Guard painted Green half Circular

MR MACNAUGHTON, 1809–11

Two Brass Fire Guards. A Brass wire Fender. A Set of Polished Steel Fire Irons with Gilt Stars

A Strong Brass Framed hanging Fire Guard

Two handsome Brass Circular Guards

A Brass Guard with Rails Mounted on Pillars with Tripods

A Circular Fire Guard Painted Green with Brass Rim

FIRE IRONS

MR HOPKINS, 1808

A Set of Fire Irons

MR TURNER, 1808

A handsome Set of Fire irons pollished Steel ingraved with Royal Arms

MR MACNAUGHTON, 1809–10

Three Pair of Steel Standards for receiving Fire Irons

Three Pair of Steel Fire Iron Standards

MR FELTHAM, 1812

A Small Range, Poker, Tongs and Shovel

CUTLER & MACNAUGHTON, 1812

A Pair of Blocks & Standard made of Pollished Steel for to receive the Fire Irons

GRATES

MR HOPKINS, 1807–08
The Body, Front, and Grate
Two Pollished Steel Grate Fronts, Two Fenders, Two Sets of Fire Irons

MR FELTHAM, 1808
A Steel Fronted Grate Gothic ornaments

MR MACNAUGHTON, 1809–11
The Fronts of Two Grates Gilt Ornaments in Front, on Morone Colourd ground.
Two handsome Grate Fronts finished with Morone Japan pannels and Silver Stars with polished Steel margins
A Steel Fronted Grate with Gilt mouldings to the Pannels
A Grate with Dark Brown Pannels and Gilt ornaments, A Steel Fender with Gilt ornaments and Standards, a Set of Fire Irons.
The Front of a Grate morone Colour and Gilt ornaments
A New Grate with japan morone Front with Gilt half Collomns and Honey Suckle Gilt Border
A very handsome Grate with Gilt Pillars and other Gilt ornaments
A Fender and Fire Irons
A grate with morone Front with Gilt mouldings and Gilt Roses A Fender and Fire Irons to Correspond.
A handsome Steel Fronted Grate with Or Molu ornaments with Standard Fender to Correspond with the Grate. A set of Fire Irons

MESSRS CUTLER, 1814
A New Grate, bright Steel Front with Brass or Gilt mouldings, Iron Body fitted up with Retort pipes and 6 side Gilt Patterns for the admission of Hot Air into the Room (For the Prince Regents Bed Room)

STOVES

MR HOPKINS, 1807–09
A Steel Fronted Stove with Brass Fasces and Battle Axes, A fender and fire irons
A Bath Stove and Fire Irons, A Shovel & Tongs
Three Bath Stoves

MR FELTHAM, 1811–12
Two Bath Stoves
Two Circular Fire Guards Painted Green with Brass Rims
A Large Strong Rumford Stove

MR MACNAUGHTON, 1812
An Iron Pedestal Stove

MR CUTLER, 1820
A New Stove with projecting Bars & Sloping Iron Top to assist the Draft.
A Wire Fender Painted Yellow & Brass Rim

COAL SCUTTLES

MR FELTHAM, 1811–14
Two Japan Coal Scuttles
3 Copper Coal Hods

THOMASON & JONES, BIRMINGHAM, 1819
12 Copper Coal Scuttles

HEARTH BRUSHES

MR ODWAY, 1812
Two Laquerd Hearth Brushes

'SUITES OF CHIMNEY ORNAMENTS'

The term 'garniture de cheminée' was used in France to describe a set of objects for the adornment of the chimneypiece but it does not seem to have been much used in 18th century England; instead they might have been called 'Suites of chimney-ornaments'. Throughout this period there were two concurrent themes, one classical, the other oriental. In its classical form the garniture consisted generally of busts or vases either singly or in combination. While the idea of using furniture and shelves for the display of plate goes back to the Middle Ages, the appearance of vases and busts on chimneypieces probably dates from the Renaissance when architects, particularly in the colder climate of northern Europe, were supplying designs for chimney pieces which were effectively architecture in miniature, and were evidently considered as such — Thomas Chippendale described his classical designs as 'Two Chimney-Pieces in Architecture . . .'. So they were either articulated by one (or more) of the classical orders of columns or at least governed by their proportions. Vases or busts as points of emphasis on a skyline of a building, and figures in the form of supporting caryatids, had long been familiar to architects working in the classical style and took their place equally in the design of chimney pieces. Jean le Pautre added vases or busts explicitly to the chimneypiece (Fig. 72), so that about the time of the Restoration in England some of the principal ways of treating the shelf were known from widely-circulating engravings.

Meanwhile, the counter-subject was beginning to unfold. Chinese porcelain, as a result of exploratory voyages, began to reach Europe in quantity during the 16th century although chiefly confined to the Iberian peninsular and the trading states of Italy. With the foundation of the European East India Companies in the early 17th century the trickle became a flood so that by the 1620s an *Imaginary Interior* by Bartholomeus van Bassen showed a set or garniture of three Chinese vases arranged atop a buffet: it could equally well have been a chimneypiece. Jean le Pautre, again, several times depicted oriental garnitures in his designs and in the drawings in which Sir Christopher Wren and his carver Grinling Gibbons collaborated — the one drawing the architecture, the other the decoration for carving — these themes were apparently interchangeable: garnitures of one or the other sort dominated throughout the period.

There are emerging some indications that the choice of a classical or oriental garniture depended on written or

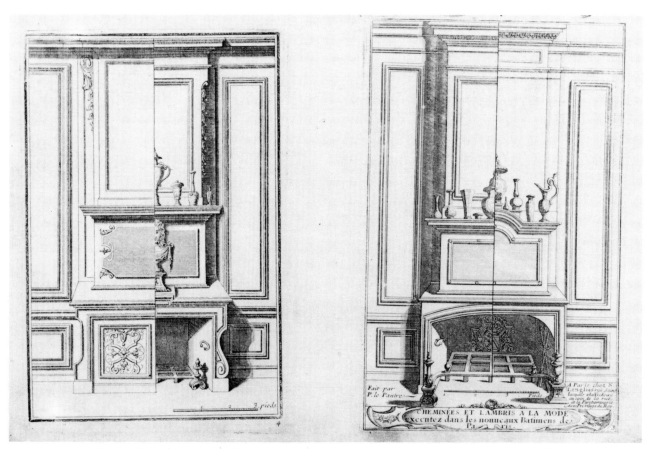

Fig. 72 Four chimneypiece designs on two plates, with garnitures, by Jean Le Pautre, after 1665

unwritten rules of etiquette about what was appropriate for what kind of room, in the same way that reception rooms or rooms of State were more formal, and more private rooms tended to be more intimate and informal. It is likely that the importance of the architect relative to the decorator (perhaps one should say carver), was another factor in this, and this balance presumably involved the house-owner too. For in rooms in which the architect played a major part — for example, in the halls at Coleshill in Berkshire in the mid 17th century, at Houghton in the 1730s or at Kedleston in the late 1760s — the 'garniture' was often conceived of as part of the architecture of the chimneypiece and is generally classical as a result, whereas in rooms in which the architect handed over the detailing to the carver or joiner, the garniture was seen as decoration rather than as architecture, and was as likely or more to be of oriental porcelain.

Another factor in deciding what kind of garniture should adorn a chimneypiece was an awareness of the symbolic significance of, for instance, the bust or figure of a classical philosopher or poet, which were soon regarded as appropriate for a library.

Throughout the second half of the 17th century and well into the 18th, Chinese porcelain, redolent of the mystery and romance of the East, maintained a great popularity. Originally made for ritual use in temples, sets of Chinese porcelain, usually numbering three, five or seven, and alternating between flaring beakers and jars or vases, were ideally suited to formal display on furniture, on the mantel-shelf and on the hearth, and rapidly became a *sine qua non* of the fashionable interior — as many as eleven items were recorded in the garniture of a room belonging to Pierre Jarosson in Paris in 1718. A wide range of Chinese and Japanese objects were recorded on chimneypieces at Burghley House in 1688.

But this was nothing to the mania for collecting Chinese porcelain that caught hold of Queen Mary and other members of the House of Orange. For them the pre-eminent Huguenot architect in exile Daniel Marot produced several designs for porcelain rooms in which ever-increasing quantities of porcelain, or European tin-glazed earthenware substitutes, were accommodated. Several examples from the Water Gallery built from 1697 at Hampton Court, whose appearance is known from engravings, survive; a porcelain room of the same period is in the Schloss Charlottenburg in Berlin. In an engraving after Eosander von Göthe's original design seven large vases are lined up on the chimneypiece and six figures, either of Blanc de Chine or monochrome porcelain, form the front row. There are numerous houses in England and in Holland in which porcelain or delftware played an important part in the decoration. The English ones include Beningbrough, Boughton, Castle Howard, Chatsworth, Drayton, Dyrham, Ham, Mereworth, Petworth and Uppark — often the chimneypiece occupied a corner position where the tiers of shelves over the chimneypiece neatly filled what might have been an awkward space. It is perhaps surprising that a spectacular house like Kiveton Park in Yorkshire, or indeed William Blathwayte's Dyrham Park, had virtually no ceramics over their fireplaces, but these were integral with the wall panelling and had a mirror and often a picture as well. (At Kiveton in 1727, for instance, the Best Dressing Room had '1 Chimney Glass fix'd in Red & Gold Japan fra. [me] 1 Whole Length of a Nun fix'd over Chimney'.) At Temple Newsam, on the other hand, inventories of 1702, 1714, 1721, 1734 and 1740 record substantial amounts of Chinese porcelain over the chimneypieces: the Drawing Room in 1734 had '80 pieces of China upon Chimney', the Mohair Room 'Some China Over Chimney (to wit) 18 pieces of different Sorts, some broke' and the Damask Room '70 Pieces of China upon the Chimney=piece & in the 2 Corners'. The 1740 inventory is more specific: '1 China punch bowl . . . 2 silver sconces, 2 China figures, 2 China bottles, 4 small China Jars, 1 small China punch bowl, 6 China basons, 2 small China potts and Covers'.

These were presumably Baroque arrangements which had survived more or less undisturbed but alterations made soon after swept all this away and scattered the components, no doubt, into other rooms in the house. The same is true of most formal Baroque garnitures. Vulnerable by their prominence, one breakage could relegate them to a china cabinet: part of a rare English delftware garniture has been identified amongst other pottery at Blair Castle in Perthshire. Chinese porcelain continued to be popular even on Palladian chimneypieces of the most severely classical character but there are signs during the 1730s and 40s of a preference for somewhat less formal arrangments. Mr and Mrs Richard Bull of Northcourt lined up eleven pieces in 1747 when they had their portrait painted by Arthur Devis but they were not a set as such: flanked by a pair of birds the pairs of lidded cups and vases centre on a seated Buddha. Hogarth splendidly satirizes the incongruity, indeed absurdity, of loading a Palladian mantel-shelf with Oriental ornaments in the second scene of his *Marriage à la Mode* (see front cover). Here a classical bust with a broken nose rises from a sea of vases and figures in assorted materials and ridiculous poses. The overmantel picture is all but hidden: the floral wall light impossibly naturalistic. A light-hearted attempt has been made to recreate such an ensemble for this exhibition.

The period of the Rococo naturally favoured Chinese porcelain for its decorative qualities and Chippendale, amongst others, provided designs for elaborate overmantel mirror frames which included places for oriental items. John Crunden topped one of his chimneypiece designs published in 1766 with eleven vases of three different sizes, each of them containing a small bunch of flowers; perhaps intended to represent European porcelain they could equally well have been Chinese (Fig. 73).

In 1770 Queen Charlotte removed the Chinese porcelain vases from her bedroom chimneypiece and replaced them with ones of classical design. Fashion was

Fig. 73 Chimneypiece and garniture by John Crunden, 'The Chimneypiece Maker's Daily Assistant', 1766, pl.33

changing and many arrangements of oriental porcelain must have been swept away in the feverishly renewed interest in classical architecture. Even the most rigorous neo-classical architects could not completely control their patrons' individual taste and oriental things crept back on the chimneypiece. Harewood House, that neoclassical showpiece, provides several examples in 1795:

> In the Coffee Room . . . one Piramid, 2 China Flower Pots 2 China Figures, and 2 Marble Figures over the Fire place . . .
> In the Breakfast Room . . . 4 Small Jars & 2 Birds over the Chimney Piece

Some of the components of these no doubt survive around the house.

When the widow of the 9th Viscount Irwin died in 1808, the inventory of Temple Newsam shows us what was on the chimneypieces, though again some of the locations are less than specific:

> Lady William Gordon's . . . 8 China jars and bottles some broke a large china jar . . .

Anti room First Floor . . . a glass over the chimney in a carved a [? gilt] frame a coloured china jar 2 blue and white Ditto 2 small ditto 5 small pieces [all presumably on the chimneypiece].

Lady Irwin's Dressing Room first floor . . . fifteen pieces of different sorts of China figures and vases on the Chimney piece 2 Cut glass candlesticks two china figures 2 light candlesticks 2 ditto setting figures 2 one light Gerandoles 2 small figures and 2 small vases . . .

It is not easy to be sure how much of all this was on the chimneypiece. There are two other things of interest here: all these rooms were those of the female members of the family (the 'Anti room' led to Lady Irwin's Dressing Room), suggesting that at this date the taste for oriental porcelain may have been a feminine one; whether the rooms were old-fashioned or, like Lady William Gordon's, had been remodelled barely ten years earlier, the impression is of assemblies rather than garnitures, mixing blue and white and enamelled pieces, some of them perhaps retrieved from what had been swept away in the alterations of the 1740s. The only oriental rather than classical ornaments in a reception room were, rather surprisingly, those on the Palladian chimneypieces in the

'Picture Gallery' or Saloon. By and large these Irwins were not quickly blown by the winds of fashion.

Lady Hertford changed all that. Her remodellings of 1827–28 were in the newest taste and brought the Jacobean-revival, perhaps the rococo revival and certainly the Regency *chinoiserie* to the house. There may well have been a formal garniture on the marble chimneypiece of her Chinese Drawing Room, for these were clearly back in vogue: Sir John Soane even had one in his bathroom in 1825.

The other strand that ran unbroken throughout the period was the classical and during the Baroque period in England the architectural character of the chimney piece often incorporating vases or a bust in the design tended to make a garniture unnecessary. These busts and vases were carved by the same man as made the chimneypiece or supplied by a sculptor such as Andrew Carpenter or John Nost, who advertised for sale in 1712 his collection of 'Marble and Leaden Figures, Busto's and Noble Vases, Marble Chimney Pieces, and Curious Marble Tables . . .'. Most of the figures and busts were of lead and must have been intended for garden ornaments, but there is no reason why some should not have been used indoors. The subjects were mostly classical but included some contemporaries or near-contemporaries. In Palladian houses a single bust was often placed on a mantelshelf, sometimes interrupting a picture hung above or the carved relief of an overmantel. This is indeed the arrangement one almost expects to find in paintings by William Hogarth, for example *Marriage à la Mode* (see front cover), *Scene from the 'Indian Emperor'* or *A reception at Wanstead*, this great house in Essex, built by Colen Campbell for Sir Richard Child about 1720, being the last word in Palladian splendour. Around this time it would have been unusual to see in England a formal arrangement of small bronzes on a chimneypiece although this would certainly have been possible on the continent from the late 17th century: Mme de Seignelay had such an arrangement in her elegant Paris house in 1693. England had no tradition of fine wood-carving as there was in Germany, where a virtuoso set of boxwood figures was produced which now forms a garniture in the Second George Room at Burghley — originally they were divided between two rooms. Nor was there a tradition of bronze-casting. So when replicas or reductions of famous classical vases, busts or figures was required either they had to be imported from France or Italy, or they had to be obtained in different materials, amongst them marble, terracotta, ivory, lead or plaster.

The demand was, in the middle years of the century, largely supplied by Henry and John Cheere, who led the field in the mass production of lead and plaster statuettes and portrait busts. Their circle included the sculptors Peter Scheemakers, who had first-hand knowledge of classical antiquities from a visit to Rome in 1728–30, Louis-Francois Roubiliac, Michael Rysbrack and Robert Taylor, the painters Francis Hayman and William Hogarth and the cabinetmaker Thomas Chippendale.

Although the busts and figures produced by the Cheeres became most popular for decorating the walls of halls, staircases and libraries, in particular, on occasion no doubt they found their way on to chimneypieces as well: in 1745–46 or perhaps twenty years later no fewer than fifteen plaster busts were supplied to Temple Newsam — some crowned the cornice of the Palladian library which had, in 1808, 'A plaister bronze figure on the chimney piece'; that same year there were '2 white painted plaster heads on the chimneypiece' in the Great Hall (Cat. 68).

The makers of these decorative plasters depended heavily on contemporary sculptors, and the modellers in the leading English porcelain factories in their turn depended on the plaster-makers, adapting Cheere plaster figures to the Rococo style by the addition of rock-work bases. In the 1760s, for instance, the Bow factory produced their own version of the Farnese Flora, based on a Rysbrack terracotta available in plaster from John Cheere, and the Derby factory did the same with their Milton and Shakespeare. These porcelain figures may have been intended as table ornaments but there is evidence of their use as garnitures on chimneypieces. Garnitures of vases, of sinuous profile and elaborate floral decoration, represented the modification of the classical vase shape to conform to the mid 18th century rococo fashion.

In less than a generation the neoclassical style took hold, and the demand for vases, busts and statuettes for chimney-garnitures was increasingly met by Josiah Wedgwood, who had perfected his 'black basaltes' material by 1769. This fine stoneware material was cheaper than bronze and more satisfactory, both in durability and quality of reproduction, than the Cheere plasters which one way or another Wedgwood and Gentley contrived to copy. In 1781 Wedgwood sold off his stock of decorative wares after the death of Thomas Bentley the year before. The Christie and Ansell catalogue records 'STATUES, FIGURES, SMALL BUSTS, CANDELABRA *and* LAMPS, disposed into Suites for CHIMNEY-ORNAMENTS'. Here are some typical lots, with the prices they realized:

> 67 A Suite of seven Pieces; the Center, a chased Lamp, forming a Tripod with Etruscan Sphinxes, two Egyptian Lions, two Griffin Candelabra [£2 15s]
>
> 677 7: [pieces] Bust of Venus, 2 boys, 2 beakers with Etruscan borders, pr Egyptian Sphinx Candelabra [£4 6s 6d]
>
> 874 . . . a Vase for a Watch-case, a Pair of Busts, two Sphinx Candelabra

These lots, of co-ordinating objects, were 'disposed into suites' by Wedgwood but owners could do the same for themselves, as the anonymous man and woman in a well-known painting at Temple Newsam clearly did: on their chimneypiece is a pair of Griffin candelabra and a copy of the Capitoline Flora (Cat. 69). In black basaltes this garniture would have cost something under £2 in total, rather less per item than the average of £1 12s for John Cheere's plaster statuettes, and a fraction of the £9 9s that Lord Boringdon paid for a bronze statuette of the Farnese Flora by the Zoffoli brothers in Rome in the 1790s. These bronze-like basaltes garnitures were evidently very chic. In 1795 Harewood House had '2 black Wedgwood Sphinks . . .' in the Billiard Room, '4 Wedgwood Vauses upon the Chimney Pieces . . .' in the great Hall and '6 busts, 5 Black Figures upon the Chimney Piece' in the Library.

Some patrons were prepared to go to the expense of buying bronzes in Rome. Lord Boringdon of Saltram was one. He bought seven items from the Zoffoli brothers in Rome, among them reductions of the Medici vase, the Borhese vase, Marcus Aurelius, Agrippina and Menander. Sir Lawrence Dundas also preferred the real thing and most of the *garniture de cheminée* in the Library at 19 Arlington Street, London, (well-known from Zoffany's painting) survives in the collection of the Marquess of Zetland. Some unlikely materials were pressed into service to provide substitutes for expensive bronzes, one of the most unlikely of which was coal: in 1769 Robert Towne made some vases of cannel coal, which takes a high polish, for the chimneypiece in the dining room at Burton Constable. Designed by Timothy Lightoler, an unknown number of these cost £17 1s: one survives. The same year, 1769, that Wedgwood perfected his black basaltes, Mrs Coade also introduced her substitute for marble, bronze and plaster, an artificial stone which was a patent fired ceramic material. *Coade's Gallery or Exhibition in Artificial Stone*, 1799, indicates that some of her products were intended as ornaments on the chimneypiece and a pair of candelabra has recently been acquired for Heaton Hall, Manchester (Cat. 73): one is dated 1795. Their comparatively unsophisticated modelling and surface, together with their greater cost — in the region of four or five guineas each — prevented them from seriously rivalling black basaltes and Coade stone garnitures or lamps rarely appears in contemporary inventories. The almost universal placing of candelabra or lamps at either end of a neoclassical chimney piece is illustrated at Woodhall Park in Hertfordshire where the Print Room, 'D'sign'd & Finished by R. Parker 1782', has the nice conceit of engravings of candlesticks where real ones would appear.

The number of other materials used to satisfy the taste for garnitures in the classical style is very considerable. Around 1764–68 a suite of three creamware vases was supplied to Saltram (probably by Wedgwood), their engine-turned bodies closely resembling the virtuoso exercises of turning in ivory practised by many aristrocrats during the 18th century, a collection of which is at Rosenborg Slot in Copenhagen. Wedgwood's 1781 catalogue also lists garnitures in painted Etruscan ware, Jasper ware and 'in imitation of CHRYSTALLINE STONES', three of which remain at Saltram. For example:

19 A set of five, Granite; the two end Vases serving for Candelabra [£2 11s]

22 A set of seven, Egyptian Pebble [£2]

1125 A suite of five, the Centre designed for a Watch-case [£6]

This last is one of only two references in the catalogue to time-pieces being placed on the chimneypiece. The following year, 1782, the Derby porcelain factory offered for sale a garniture of five vases painted in enamel colours, and two such sets survive: their striking colours probably bring together those of the interiors for which they were bought and provide invaluable evidence for the original brilliance of these colours.

When Queen Charlotte removed the Chinese porcelain from her bedroom chimneypiece in 1770 what she commissioned in its stead was a set of seven vases from Matthew Boulton, the most successful manufacturer of ormolu (gilt bronze) in England. From this moment onwards ormolu played as important a part on the English chimneypiece as it had already done in France for more than a hundred years. The royal commission was executed in his favourite material, Derbyshire fluorspar or Blue John, the name deriving from the French, *bleu-jaune*, and several of the component vases are still in existence, four of them now flanking Boulton's King's Clock in a garniture at Windsor Castle. Other materials available in his ormolu mounts were white and black marble, earthenware, porcelain, glass and enamelled copper. Ormolu was, of course, a particularly suitable material for the branches of candelabra and these feature regularly in contemporary views, from the end of the 18th century usually flanking a clock. By the early 19th century all three items were becoming so elaborate that they were covered by glass domes — several are visible in views of the Royal Pavilion at Brighton. At the same time ormolu was used for the manufacture of new forms of lighting used on the chimneypiece: a pair of handsome colza-oil lamps (Cat. 76) made for one of the grand Regency interiors of Clumber Park, the country house of the Duke of Newcastle, may have been used on a chimneypiece.

So far, attention has been focused largely on the formal, symmetrical arrangements of mathing objects forming the *garniture de cheminée* but in less public rooms or during the course of everyday life the chimneypiece provided a convenient flat surface to use as we would today. So contemporary views show a pair of bellows momentarily laid down on an otherwise empty shelf, a coffee pot, a candlestick brought to provide more light, letters, ribbons. One even serves as a perch for a pet parrot. Invitations or theatre tickets are tucked into the frames of rococo or neoclassical overmantel mirrors, much as socialites do today: in the Duchesse de Berry's private drawing room at the Tuileries in the 1820s there are literally dozens of them. Informality was always more likely in middle-class than in artistocratic surroundings. But the Duchesse de Berry leant small framed pictures up

SUITES OF CHIMNEY ORNAMENTS 77

on her mantelpiece in just the same way as Admiral Bosanquet did with silhouettes of his family in the drawing room of his modest house at Clay Hill, Enfield, in 1843; and the publisher John Murray did the same at 50 Albermarle Street, London. Silhouettes also play a part in an asymmetrical arrangement of oriental and western objects on the chimneypiece of the Duke of Wellington's Study at Apsley House around 1850, an arrangement which accords nicely with present-day tastes for studied imbalance. In both formal and informal arrangements new things make their appearance on chimneypieces. Hand-held face-screens to protect the face and make-up from the heat of the fire had been hung from a hook on or beside the chimneypiece as early as the 1740s but from the Regency they began to be leant up on the mantel-shelf, as in the drawing room of the 2nd Earl of Dunraven at Adare Manor in Co. Limerick, and this was done on the continent as well. A pair of these face-screens is visible in an early photograph among the other ornaments on one of the chimneypieces in the Long Gallery at Temple Newsam. Other objects that occasionally found their way on to mantel-shelves included tobacco boxes and spill vases which enabled owners to light their candles, or pipes, from the glowing coals in the grate. By the middle of the 19th century, therefore, the decoration of chimneypieces had become extremely elaborate, pairs of disparate objects being used together almost indiscriminately: a view of the Dining Room at Balmoral in 1855 shows a clock framed by pairs of cups, probably of ruby glass, 'Greek' vases, tazze perhaps of porphyry, and bronze figurines. What would Rudolf Ackermann have made of this when he had written thirty years before 'In [the illustration] there are four articles that were not unfrequently placed together, as accident might produce the assemblage: the chimney-piece was bought at the mason's — the grate at the smith's — the frame at the carver's — and the lock, any where so that it was from Paris — all ready-made, all differing in style, and all unlike in composition and execution. Instead of this *melange* of conflicting parts a uniform whole is now studied, and propriety and suitableness established in its place'.

By far the most elusive decorations of the chimneypiece are flowers. Because of their transitory nature they are not, of course, recorded in inventories and only sometimes occur in contemporary views, depending to some extent, no doubt, on the time of the year. There are indications, however, that they were as popular in the 18th and 19th centuries as they are today for bringing the scent and colour of the flower garden indoors. Around the middle of the 18th century they turn up everywhere: at Temple Newsam they decorate the entire Saloon in needlework upholstery on the suite supplied by James Pascall. Flowers were associated with the chimneypiece specifically, as we have seen, by being placed in vases on the hearth in summer, appearing on chimney boards and in the needlework of firescreens. On the chimney they were placed in the most extensive garnitures, and when

they could not be fresh they were dried or artificial — made in silk, paper, straw, glass, ormolu (incorporated in candelabra), even shellwork. '2 carved Baskets of Flowers as Girandoles to hold 3 Lights each', made of carved and gilt wood, were supplied to William Weddell of Newby Hall, Yorkshire, by Thomas Chippendale for the tapestry room in the mid 1770s. Although perhaps intended for the pier tables between the windows they could equally well have served on the chimneypiece, where they are today. Either way, they correspond with the 18th-century delight in placing baskets of freshly-picked flowers around the room, which were renewed when the flowers wilted. Flowers played a particularly important part in festive occasions, geraniums or pinks, orange or rose bushes, being brought in on tables in the windows and on the chimneypiece. Their effect can be judged in 1985 at Osterley during the flower festival sponsored by the National Trust.

Wedgwood described the containers his factory made for the fireplace to Bentley in 1772: 'Ladies find that they prefer those things with spouts . . . they say that sort keep the flowers distinct and clever. Vases are furniture for a chimneypiece — Bough-pots for a hearth, under a slab or Marble Table. I think they can never be used one instead of the other and I apprehend one reason why we have not made our *dressing* flowerpots to please has been by adapting them for chimneypieces where I think they do not place any pots dress'd with flowers'. He was wrong in this — there is plenty of evidence for flowers both growing and 'dress'd' on chimneys: Harewood House had in 1795

> In the Coffee Room . . . one Piramid, 2 china Flower Pots 2 China Figures, and 2 Marble Figures over the Fire Place
>
> In the Dining Room . . . 3 Urns upon Pedestals 2 large Pyramids & 2 small Do. & 2 Flower Pots over the Chimney Piece
>
> State Bed Room . . . 4 Urns over the Chimney Piece, 13 Flower Pots & 2 Cranes & 2 Lions.

Here it is unclear whether all these were over the chimneypiece: it may be significant that flowers were placed in eating rooms.

Bulbs were also placed on the chimneypiece, hyacinths being visible in a Dutch house in 1817 and, in a specially shaped glass vase, in an illustration by George Cruik-shank, Narcissi in a French one (Praz, figs 242 and 41). In the dining room of the Ruspoli family's Italian palace Wedgwood would have been delighted to see one of his vases 'dress'd' with flowers (Cat. 71, Praz fig. 66).

66 Garniture of Chinese porcelain

Decorated with *famille verte* enamel colours, first half 18th century

Assemblies of pairs of otherwise unmatched objects are commonly seen in paintings by, for instance, Arthur

66

Devis in his portrait of Mr and Mrs Richard Bull in 1747
(Thornton 1984, pl. 146)
Occasionally all the objects might have been filled with
flowers (see fig. 73)

Leeds City Art Galleries

67

67 Garniture of three vases and two beakers
Porcelain, Chinese, probably reign of Ch'ien Lung,
c. 1790
h. 49.5 overall

Formal garnitures of Chinese porcelain regained their
earlier popularity during the late 18th and early 19th
century

Leeds City Art Galleries

68

68 Horace and Seneca
Plaster, painted white
h. 66

From a set of fifteen busts probably made by John Cheere
(1709–87) in London and supplied for the Library at
TempleNewsam, either c. 1745 when the room was
finished or in the late 1760s when John Carr, who in
1762 had used Cheere's plasters at Fairfax House in
York, was working at Temple Newsam. The Library

here, designed by Daniel Garrett, is very architectural
and if the busts were originally positioned above the
Corinthian columns, against the attic, thirteen would
have been accounted for in this way. Two may have been
moved to the Great Hall in 1796 when alterations to this
room were completed and its chimneypiece, presumably
designed by the architect William Johnson, was installed.
The 1808 inventory records '2 white painted plaister
heads on the chimney piece a wedgewood Vase'. They
were probably removed again by Lady Hertford who
seems to have had a Jacobean-style overmantel made
(Fig. 8)

Leeds City Art Galleries

69

69 Conversation picture
English school, second half 18th century
Oil on canvas, 91.3 × 73.7

An unidentified woman has paused from her needlework.
Her husband stands leaning on a two-fold fire screen
inset with panels perhaps of silk 'lustring'. There seems to
be a brass fender on the hearth, round which the carpet
has been fitted. The conventional neoclassical
chimneypiece has a pair of griffin candlesticks with a
statuette of Flora in the centre. No painting is shown over
the chimney or either side, and this may not be a real
interior for the proportions are cramped. But the
furnishing details are true to life and the objects on the
chimneypiece are not imaginary: the Flora is a reduction
in either basaltes or black-painted plaster of the antique

marble statue in the Capitoline Museum, Rome, which John Cheere is known to have produced as a life-sized plaster, the griffin candlesticks were designed by William Chambers and are known in ormolu by Matthew Boulton and in black basaltes and jasperware by Wedgwood (the original block being in the Wedgwood Museum at Barlaston). A similar pair was on the chimney piece in the Library at 13 Lincoln's Inn Field (Cornforth, fig. 117). In basaltes they probably cost around 30s new.

Leeds City Art Galleries

70

70 Pair of candelabra
Jasperware with ormolu and crystal-glass
The jasperware by Wedgwood c. 1780
h. 35.6

Each drum has three classical scenes. A. Helen, Aphrodite, Eros & Paris | Aeneas, Diomedes & Apollo | Ulysses staying the chariot of Victory, B. Bellerophon & Pegasus | Priam begging the Body of Hector | Psyche

wounded & bound by Cupids, derived from antique reliefs known to Wedgwood through engravings. The fine jasper drums were mounted as four-branch candelabra in ormolu with glass lustres to give enhanced glitter from the candles. Candelabra often incorporated artificial flowers in their design for flowers were frequently placed on the chimneypiece

Manchester City Art Galleries, Heaton Hall

71 Three flower vases
Pearlware decorated with brown slip, impressed WEDGWOOD, c. 1790
h. of tallest (lacks its lid) 22

Although catalogued by Peter Walton as potpourri vases these were actually intended for flowers and conform generally to Wedgwood's description in his Common Place Book 1: 'Bow Pots — essential Properties of —some large for hearths, under slabs, — other less and of vase forms, for chimney pieces'
The vases are made in three sections, the shoulder section pierced for individual stems. However an Italian painting, of 1807, shows a chimneypiece with an almost identical vase filled with flowers in a completely informal arrangement

Leeds City Art Galleries

71
72

72 Pair of obelisks
Staffordshire or Yorkshire, 1790s
Pearlware, decorated with coloured slips and gilt
h. 37

Obelisks appear on chimney pieces quite regularly during the neoclassical period, usually in pairs but occasionally singly. At Osterley Park in 1782 there were in the Breakfast Room: 'Three Sparr Vases and two Obelisks over the Chimney' and at Harewood in 1795 the Yellow Drawing Room had '. . . 2 Obelisks and one Urn upon the Chimney Piece . . .'. A single obelisk in a group of ornaments on a chimneypiece is visible in an 1822 watercolour of the Lower Library at Chatsworth

Leeds City Art Galleries

73 Psyche and Hymen
Coadestone, 1795
h. 47

Impressed *COADE LAMBETH* on Hymen, COADE LONDON 1795 on Psyche
These figures were modelled by the sculptor John Bacon (1740–99) and made at Eleanor Coade's factory. A pair

73

73

74

was exhibited at the Society of Artists in 1777 '183 Hymen and Psyche; two Figures for Candelabrums'. Eleanor Coade's *Descriptive Catalogue* of 1784 gives their dimensions and prices:

46 Hymen [plinth] 15 [inches by] 5½	£4 4s 0d
47 Psyche – 15 [inches by] 5½	£4 4s 0d
Ditto, fitted up with Spring Tubes for lights, each fig	£5 5s 0d

They were illustrated, one of them on a neoclassical bracket. Their use on chimneypieces was attested in *Coade's Gallery or Exhibition in Artificial Stone*, 1799, p. 33:

[in the front room . . .]

101 *An Hymen* — setting figure, bronzed, fitted up with spring tubes, wax lights

102 *A Psyche* — setting figure, bronzed, companion to the *Hymen*

N.B. These two elegant little statues are from models executed at the Manufactory by the late Mr BACON, for Mr LOCKE, to be placed on chimney-pieces.

Manchester City Galleries, Heaton Hall

74 Garniture of five vases
Rockingham works, Swinton, Yorkshire, *c.* 1828
h. 44
Porcelain decorated in underglaze blue, enamel colours and gilt, in imitation of the Japanese *Imari* style.

75

Probably made as a result of an upsurge in the popularity of chinoiserie decoration during the Regency period, one effect of which was Lady Hertford's creation of the Chinese Drawing Room at Temple Newsam in 1827–28

Leeds City Art Galleries

75 Mantel clock
White marble and ormolu, *c.* 1785
h. 53
Movement by Jean-Baptiste Lepaute, Paris
Mantel clocks seem to have been introduced in France towards the end of the 17th century (a design for the Chambre du Roi at Versailles includes one in 1684) but in England they are rarely illustrated on chimney pieces until late in the 18th century. They probably existed — Robert Adam designed a 'case for a Watch proposed to be placed upon a Table or Chimney-piece & maybe executed in Metals or in Wood gilt', and two of the suites of chimney ornaments in Wedgwood's 1781 sale included cases for watches — but French clocks may always have been preferred: during the Regency period Rudolf Ackermann wrote, considering the origins of the chimney ensemble, 'and the clock, any where so that it was from Paris'. They were often covered by glass domes to protect them from dust

Leeds City Art Galleries

76 Pair of colza-oil lamps
Ormolu and opaque glass
h. 42.5
In the form of antique rhytons with boars' head spouts supporting cylindrical wick-holders and opaque glass shades engraved with Greek key ornament. The covers of the reservoirs are engraved with a Ducal coronet over the letter N, almost certainly for the Duke of Newcastle at Clumber Park, Nottinghamshire. Clumber was a mid 18th century house altered in 1829 by Sidney Smirke (and demolished *c.* 1938); the lamps may have been associated with Smirke's alterations. They have punched numerals I and III, so four or even more may originally have been made, probably by Thomas Messenger of Birmingham and London; formerly a maker of furniture mounts, Messenger was first listed as a lamp maker in London in 1826–27 (information kindly supplied by Clive Wainwright). Their design is based on Piranesi's engraving of a funerary monument from the *Vasi* of 1778.
They were designed to burn colza or cole-seed oil which was refined from sea-kale or rape. A valve operated by a rod in the lid of the reservoirs regulated the flow of oil to the wick, controlling the intensity of light produced. Despite their comparative efficiency, oil lamps did not displace candles entirely because their light was considered unnecessarily bright, indeed harsh and even bad for the eyes

Leeds City Art Galleries

76

Buy a Fork or a Fire Shovel from *The Cryes of the City of London* (first printed in 1687) by Marcellus Laroon the elder